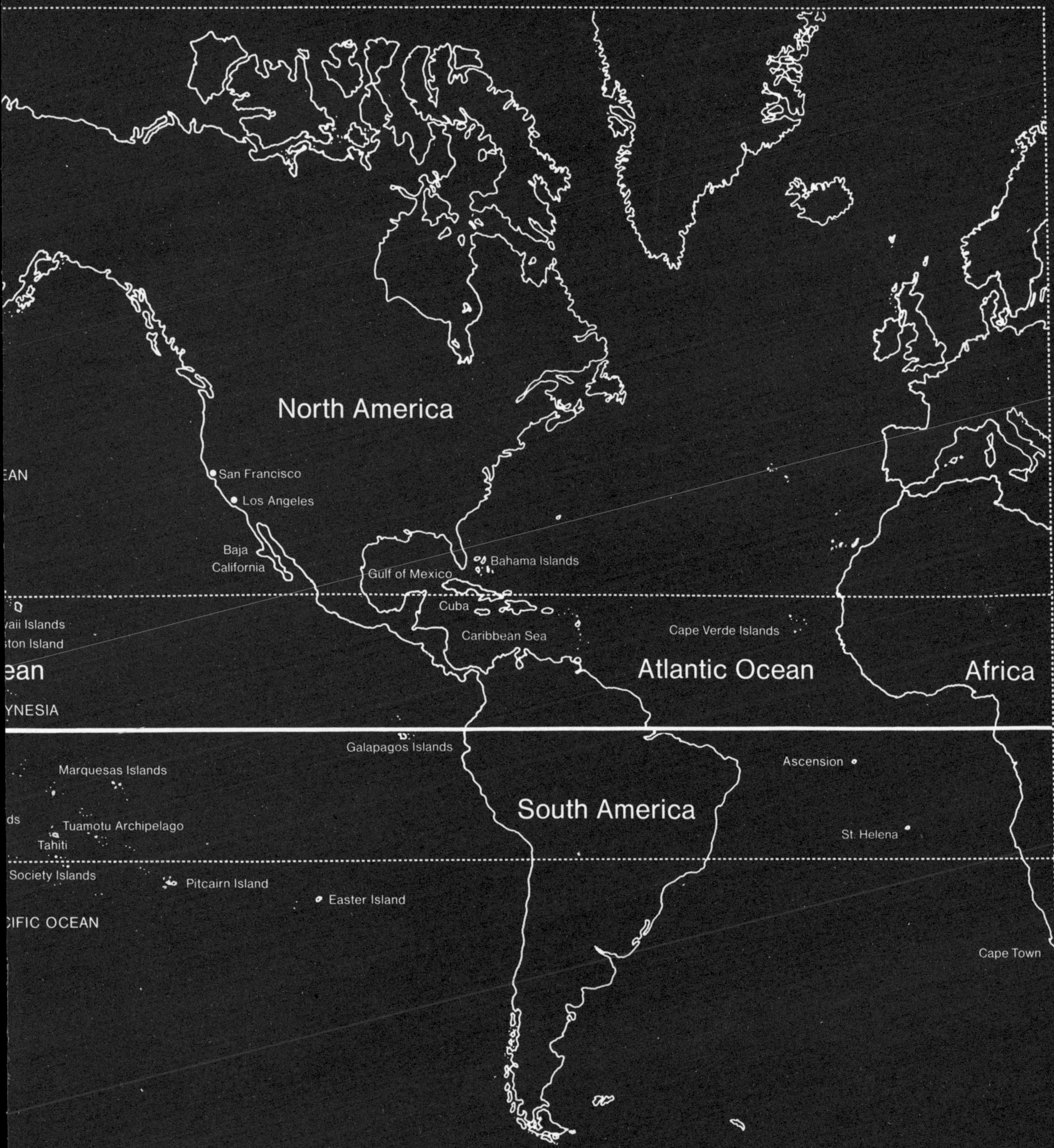

North America

EAN

San Francisco

Los Angeles

Baja California

Gulf of Mexico

Bahama Islands

Cuba

Caribbean Sea

vaii Islands

ston Island

ean

YNESIA

Cape Verde Islands

Atlantic Ocean

Africa

Galapagos Islands

Marquesas Islands

South America

Ascension

ds

Tuamotu Archipelago

Tahiti

St. Helena

Society Islands

Pitcairn Island

Easter Island

CIFIC OCEAN

Cape Town

Jacket photos

top left: *Chaetodon rainfordi*
top right: *Genicanthus watanabei*
bottom photo: *Chaetodontoplus duboulayi*

Roger C. Steene

Butterfly and Angelfishes of the World

Volume 1
Australia

Dedicated to
Dr. Gerald Allen
Ichthyologist,
my diving buddy and
teacher

Pickersgill Reef,
Part of the Australian
Great Barrier Reef,
at low tide.

Library of Congress Cataloging in Publication Data

Steene, Roger C.
Butterfly and angelfishes of the world.
"A Wiley-Interscience publication."
Bibliography: p.
Includes indexes.
CONTENTS: v. I. Australia.
1. Chaetodontidae. 2. Marine aquarium fishes.

I. Title.

QL638.C48S74 1978 597'.58 78-17351

ISBN 0-471-04737-6

Artwork: H. J. Braun, Grafic Design Studio, Werther, W. Germany
Typesetting: Frommeyer, Osnabrück, W. Germany
Printing: MERGUS Press, Hongkong
Lithography: MWK-Repro GmbH, Kirchlengern, W. Germany
Editor: Dr. Gerald R. Allen, Perth, Australia
Aquaristic Revision: Hans A. Baensch, Melle, W. Germany

First Edition in English 1978

Printed in Hongkong

Roger C. Steene

Butterfly and Angelfishes of the World

Volume 1
Australia

A Complete Survey of the Species
of Australia and New Guinea.
As Well As Their Occurrence
in the Indo-Pacific Region.
Including 236 Colour Illustrations
With More Than 100 Original
Underwater Photos.

Aquaristic Revision
Hans A. Baensch

A WILEY-INTERSCIENCE PUBLICATION
JOHN WILEY & SONS, New York · Toronto · Chichester · Brisbane

Contents

Foreword

An extensive, excellently illustrated book about the most beautiful coralfishes – the butterfly and the angelfishes – has never been published before.
The first volume contains more than 100 underwater pictures of all the species from the coastal waters of Australia and New Guinea. Fishes of the western part of New Guinea (West Irian) will be described in volume 2.
Roger Steene, the autor of this book, gives us an impressive view of the feeding habits and the behaviour of his favourites.
Most probably, the chaetodonts developed in the early stages of the Tertiary Period (approximately 50–60 million years ago) in the region of the Indo-Australian Archipelago, from where they spread over the entire tropical coral areas of the world.
This book contains descriptions and photos of approximately 50 % of the world's chaetodontids and pomacanthids and gives virtually complete coverage for the Australia-New Guinea region.
Volume 2 (in preparation) will describe the remaining butterfly and angelfishes, especially those from the Caribbean, the Red Sea and from those areas of the Pacific that have not yet been completely investigated.
Some species, mentioned in volume 1, have never been photographed before, a fact which will make this book especially interesting and valuable for the aquarist, diver and lover of nature.
Volume 2 will appear in 1979.

Hans A. Baensch
Publisher

Acknowledgements

I have been fortunate to work with two of the world's foremost authorities on reef fishes, Dr. John E. Randall of the Bernice P. Bishop Museum, Hawaii and Dr. Gerald R. Allen of the Western Australian Museum. I sincerely thank them for their assistance, advice and encouragement.
My grateful thanks to John Braun, Alan Briggs, Wade Doak, Dr. Robert Goldstein, Dr. Douglas Hoese, Barry Hutchins, Rudie H. Kuiter, Roger Lubbock, Rolly McKay, Roy O'Connor, Steve Parish, Barry Russell, and the late Gilbert Whitley. Also to Dr. John Paxton of the Australian Museum for allowing me to examine specimens under his care.
A special thank you to Paul Watson, master of the vessel "Noremac" for enabling me to accompany him on countless expeditions to the Great Barrier Reef, many to areas never before explored.

Roger C. Steene

Introduction

The popularity enjoyed by skin diving and the keeping of marine aquarium fishes has accounted for an ever increasing interest in the identification and classification of coral reef fishes. Among the most beautiful of all reef fishes are the chaetodontids and pomacanthids, popularly known as the butterflyfishes and angelfishes or sometimes collectively called coralfishes. These highly ornate animals are characterised by a flattened, disc-like body shape and frequently the snout is elongated, enabling them to retrieve food from places which are inaccessable to other species. The angelfishes possess a long spine on each cheek which distinguishes them from the closely related butterflyfishes. These are perhaps the most exotic of all reef dwellers.

The Australia-New Guinea region represents one of the richest areas in the world with regard to its coral reef fauna. No specific work dealing with the butterfly and angelfishes of this combined region has been published to date. Munro's "Fishes of New Guinea" is the most comprehensive treatment. He includes descriptions of 41 species; however, two of these are invalid. *Chaetodon dahli,* described from three tiny juveniles is most certainly the young of a previously described form and *C. miliaris,* falsely reported from many localities in the Indo-Pacific, is found only in the Hawaiian Islands.

The present publication increases the number of chaetodontids and pomacanthids known from New Guinea from 39 to 58. In addition, 77 species belonging to these groups are reported from Australian waters. Prior to this work only 41 species were known from this large island-continent. One of these, *Chaetodon aphrodite* Ogilby, which was previously recorded from Australia, was recently shown to be the juvenile stage of *C. flavirostris* by Dr. B. Goldman. Another species, *C. vitulus,* described by Whitley from the Sydney area on the basis of juvenile specimens is probably synonymous with a known form, perhaps *C. güntheri.*

Of interest to scientists as well as the layman are records of hybrid butterflyfishes and angelfishes.

In addition, several names of well-known species have been up-dated. Many of these names have not previously appeared in print and I am indebted to Warren E. Burgess of New Jersey, USA, for furnishing this information. Mr. Burgess is a recognized authority on these fishes and is currently revising the classification of the world's butterflyfishes. The following generic names, recognized by many earlier authors, are herein included in the genus *Chaetodon: Anisochaetodon, Gonochaetodon, Megaprotodon,* and *Tetrachaetodon.*

There is still a great deal to be learned concerning spawning, growth, migration, and feeding habits of coral fishes. Where this information does exist I have included it under the appropriate section in the text.

I have also endeavoured to illustrate the different colour changes which take place in certain species during their development. Lengths given under each illustration or in the text refer to the total length unless specified as standard length (distance from tip of snout to the base of the middle rays of the caudal fin).

In addition to the butterflyfishes and angelfishes, I have included several species belonging to closely related families, most of which were erroneously included with the butterflyfishes by the naturalists of the last century. These fishes which include the scats, halfmoons, and the old wife are conspicuously marked and thus frequently come to the attention of divers and aquarists.

Because of the popularity and conspicuous habits of the butterfly and angelfishes, the chances of finding a previously undescribed species are indeed remote. However, several new deep-dwelling species have been discovered in recent years by scubadivers and there is always the possibility that others remain undetected. For example, I recently encountered a pair of unrecognizable *Chaetodon* at Haggerstone Island on the northern Great Barrier Reef. Unfortunately I was unable to collect them and their true status remains a mystery. If any readers should come across species from New Guinea and Australia which do not appear in this volume I would welcome their correspondence.

Roger Steene
Letters for Mr. Steene will be forwarded
by Mergus Verlag
Bergstrasse 3, Melle, W. Germany

Features of a typical pomacanthid fish

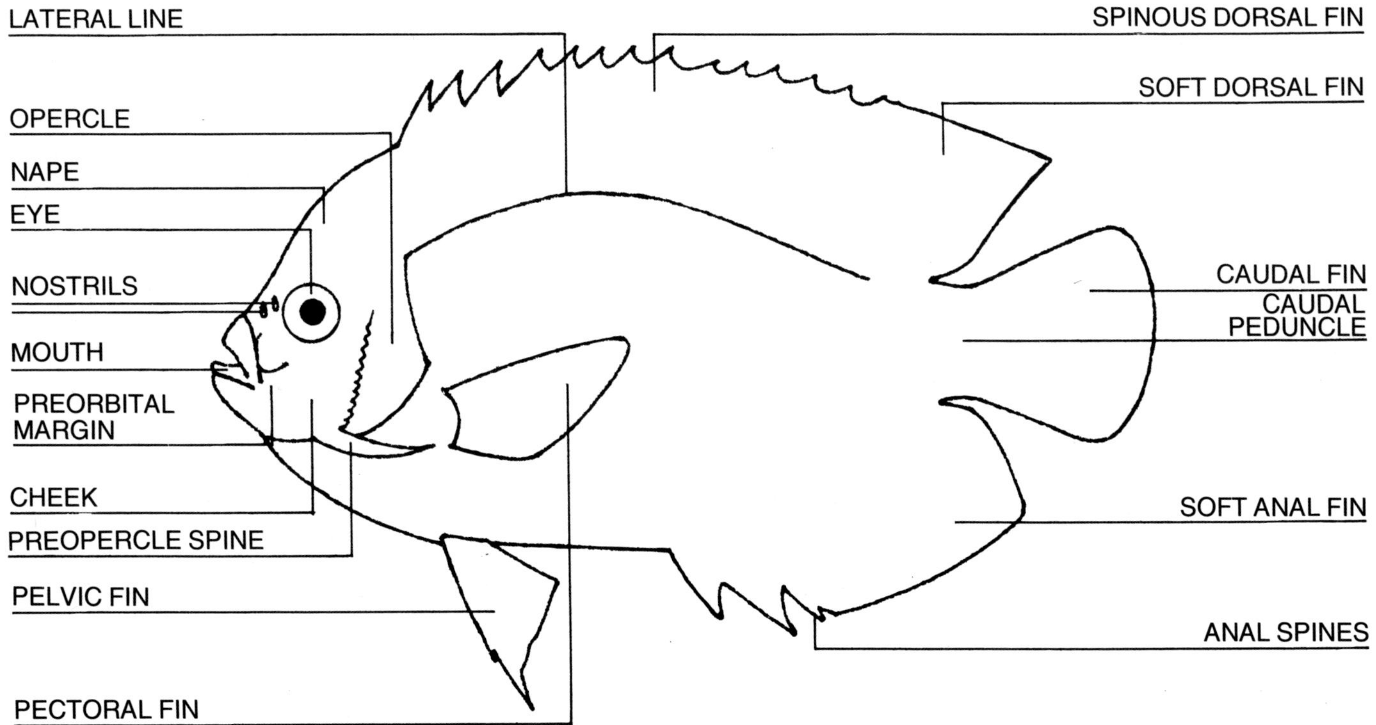

Family
Chaetodonthidae

Phylogenetic Tree of the Genera of the Sub-Family Chaetodontinae (According to AHL, 1923)

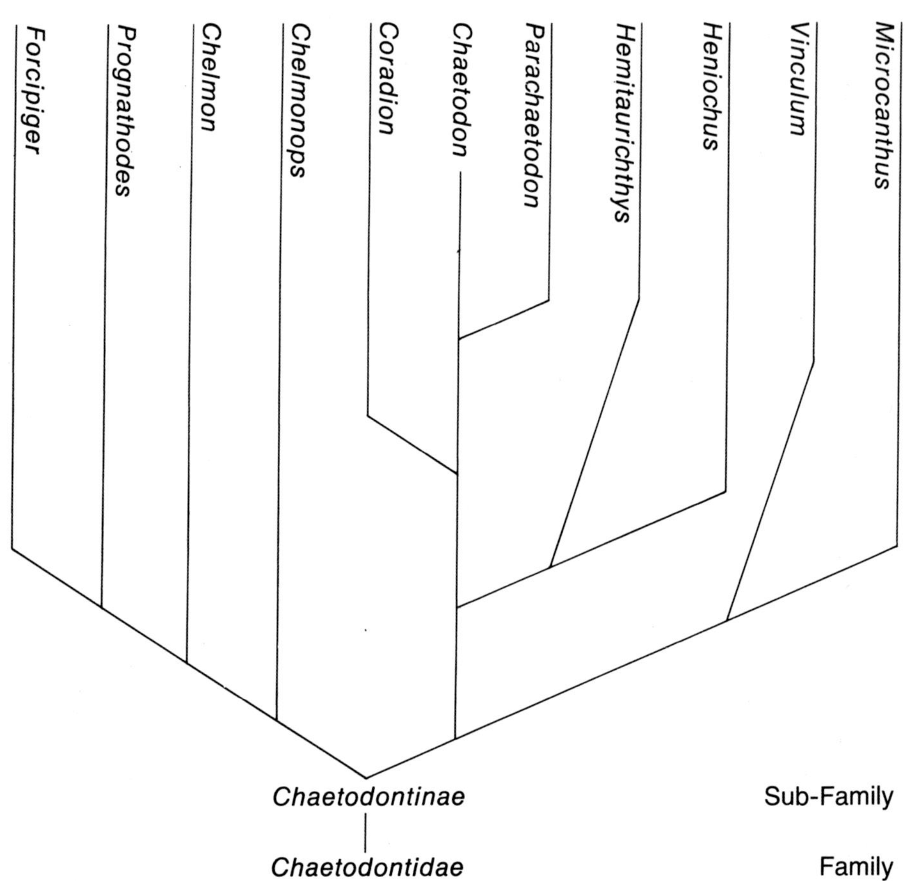

New Classification

The sub-family Chaetodontinae is no longer recognized. The family Chaetodontidae – until now including both the sub-family Chaetodontinae and sub-family Pomacanthinae – should be regarded as the sole family for butterflyfishes. Angelfishes on the other hand are now recognized as an independent familiy, Pomacanthidae.

Microcanthus and Vinculum had been included in the Chaetodontidae according to AHL; they are, however, now considered to be members of the familiy Scorpididae.

Prognathodes, a Caribbean genus of the family Chaetodontidae will be described in volume 2.

The remaining genera in AHL's Phylogenetic tree are currently considered to be valid. The phylogeny of the Pomacanthidae will be discussed in volume 2.

Genus
Chaetodon

Butterflyfishes

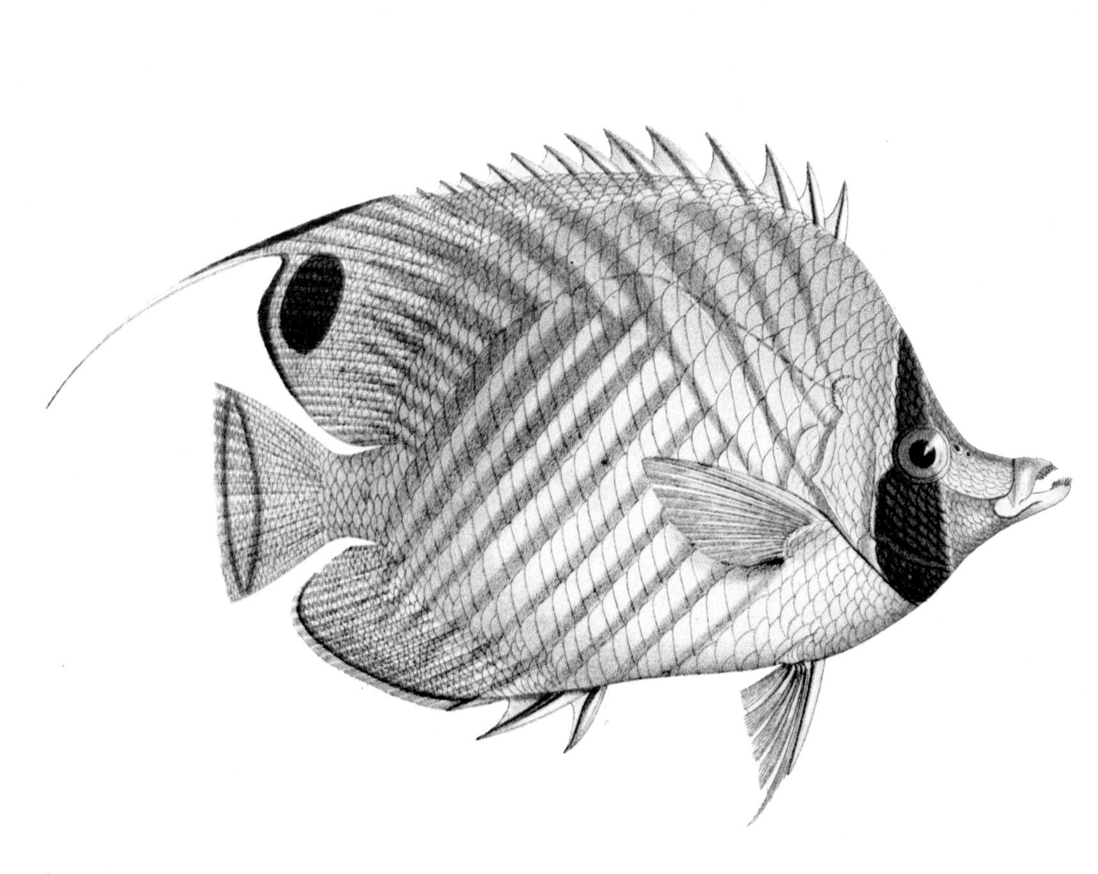

Chaetodon auriga

Chaetodon adiergastos SEALE, 1910

Philippine Butterflyfish

The Philippine Butterflyfish is rare in Australian waters. It is known only from a few specimens collected off Western Australia in the Dampier Archipelago. These were encountered at depths of between 2 and 10 metres (6 and 33 ft.), in coral reef areas. It is an extremely wary species and hence difficult to approach. The maximum size is approximately 6 inches (15 cm). This fish was previously known only from Taiwan and the Philippines, but in addition it has recently been taken at Indonesia. The Philippine Butterflyfish has seldem been imported, although it can be easily maintained in a tank.

1.
Chaetodon adiergastos
Approximately 2.75 in. (7 cm).
The ocellus disappears as the fish grows.

2.
Chaetodon adiergastos
Approximately
4 in. (10 cm).

1 ▲

2 ▼

Chaetodon assarius WAITE, 1905
Western Butterflyfish

This species is a close relative of *Chaetodon güntheri* from Southeast Australia. It is confined to Western Australia, ranging from the Perth area to Shark Bay. At the former localities it is usually sighted in depths between 1 and 12 metres (3 and 40 ft.). The Western Butterfly is a schooling fish as an adult and reaches a maximum length of about 5 inches (12.5 cm).
The diet is comprised mainly of algae and planktonic animals.
The Western Butterflyfish is unknown to American and European aquarists, although it is easily maintained in a tank, according to Australian hobbyists.

3.
Chaetodon assarius
Sub-adult
2.5 in. (6 cm).

▼ 3.

Chaetodon aureofasciatus MACLEAY, 1878
Golden-striped Butterflyfish

Found only in Australia and New Guinea, this fish is common on inner and coastal reefs of the Great Barrier Reef and is also found in coastal waters of northern New South Wales, Western Australia, and Northern Territory. It grows to 5 inches (12.5 cm), photo 4, and retains the same basic colouration and markings from the juvenile to the adult stage. Generally a shallow dwelling species, it occurs either solitarily or in pairs, picking at polyps and algae in sheltered waters. In the latter months of the year, juveniles as small as one-half inch (1.25 cm) long can be readily found among finger-type corals. Photo 6 shows a young fish of approximately 1 inch (2.5 cm). This species is able to tolerate relatively high percentages of freshwater and is frequently encountered in coastal areas in the vicinity of river mouths. Unfortunately, however, it has not yet invaded the tanks of North-American or European aquarists. According to the Australian hobbyists this species is very difficult to maintain in a tank. Worms – *Galiolaria hystrix* – are willingly accepted and after a period of adaptation, *C. aureofasciatus* may be offered enchytrae as well as "feeding-stones".

Photo 5. This unique cross between *C. aureofasciatus* and *C. rainfordi* was collected in 3 metres (10 ft.) depth at Decapolis Reef, 12 miles west of Lizard Island on the Great Barrier Reef. It was found in the company of two *C. aureofasciatus*. The fish was observed for two hours and during this period exhibited an unusual degree of boldness, being totally unafraid of my presence. A second specimen has since been sighted under the wharf at Green Island, North Queensland.
Hybridization is extremely rare in marine fishes. Approximately 30 cases have been observed, several of which involve butterflyfishes and angelfishes. A scientific paper was published by Randall, Allen, and the author which describes five of these butterflyfish crossings. In addition, the author has observed what appears to be a hybrid of *C. ornatissimus* and *C. meyeri* near Rabaul, New Britain.

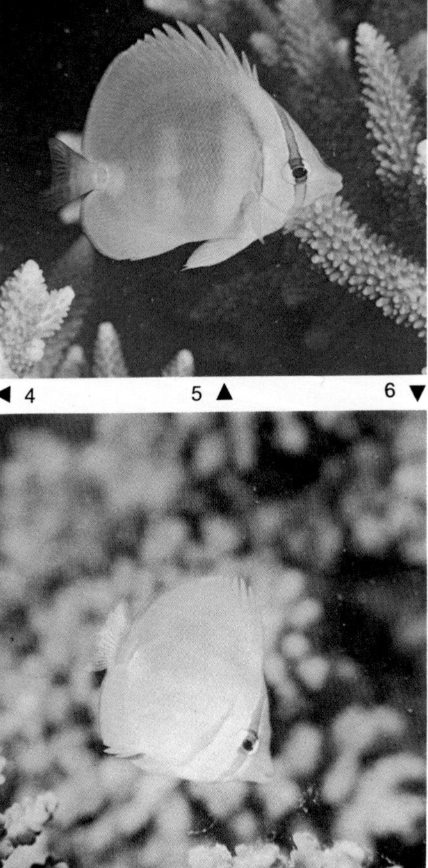

◄ 4 5 ▲ 6 ▼

Chaetodon auriga FORSKÅL, 1775
Threadfin Butterflyfish

One of the more common butterflyfishes of the Australia-New Guinea region, where it inhabits both inner and outer reefs. It has been recorded from coastal waters of New South Wales, Queensland, and Western Australia, as well as the entire Indo-Pacific. Although the Threadfin prefers areas of rich coral growth, it has also been found in regions with sparse coral. The maximum adult size is 9 inches (23 cm) and at this stage the fish has a long pennant type filament extension of the dorsal fin. It is found singly and in pairs at depths ranging from 1—10 metres (3—33 feet). Schools or groups are only occasionally observed. This species is generally bold and easy to photograph or to collect. Coral polyps, polychaetes, algae, shrimp, gastropods, and nemertine worms comprise a significant portion of the diet. This butterflyfish is also known under the sub-specific name of *C. auriga setifer.* Another sub-species, *C. auriga auriga,* has been recorded from the Red Sea. Adult specimens lack the characteristic juvenile ocellus on the dorsal fin.

7.
Chaetodon auriga
Juvenile, 1.5 in. (3.8 cm). The ocellus does not disappear with age, the extension of the dorsal fin develops in mature specimens only.

8.
Chaetodon auriga
The lower body bars are interrupted, a common variation.

9.
Chaetodon auriga
Adult specimen, 8 in. (20 cm). Underwater photo from the Great Barrier Reef.

7 ▲ 8 ▼ 9 ▶

Chaetodon baronessa CUVIER, 1831
Triangular Butterflyfish

This butterflyfish has usually been referred to as *Chaetodon triangulum.* However, there are actually two closely related fishes and the species from Australia-New Guinea, which lacks the dark, yellow-edged triangular marking on the tail (see photo 10), is *C. baronessa.* It grows to 6 inches (15 cm) and generally is seen in pairs, usually in depths less than 10 metres (33 ft.). It is a highly compressed and deep-bodied fish which allows it to slip into hiding places readily. It is usually timid and retreats even before other fish react. It is common on the Great Barrier Reef and throughout Melanesia. A few specimens have also been collected along the north coast of New South Wales.

The Triangular Butterflyfish is a delicate species which is both difficult to transport and maintain for any length of time in an aquarium.

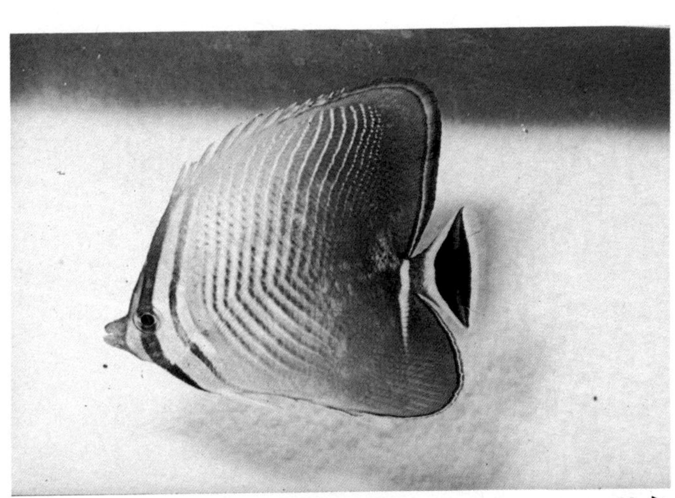

10.
For comparison:
Chaetodon triangulum
Sub-adult,
3 in. (8 cm).
This photo was taken in a tank at Sri Lanka.

10 ▲ 11 ▼ 12 ▶

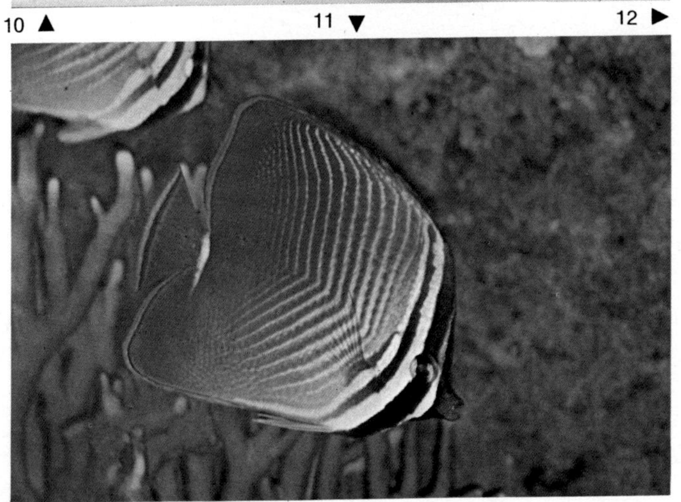

11.
Chaetodon baronessa
Adult, 5 in. (13 cm).
Underwater photo from the Great Barrier Reef.

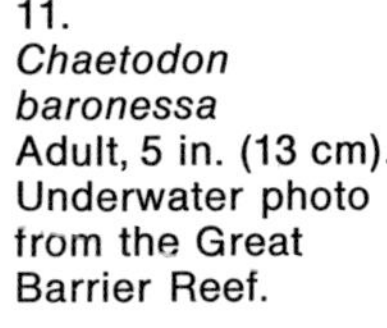

12.
Chaetodon baronessa
Juvenile,
1.5 in. (4 cm).
Underwater photo from New Guinea.

Chaetodon baronessa on the Barrier Reef

Chaetodon bennetti CUVIER, 1831
Bennett's Butterflyfish

13 ▲ 14 ▼

Not a common fish in the region, this shy species is largely confined to outer reefs in areas of heavy coral growth. The normal depth range is between 1 and 20 metres (3 and 66 feet). Two-inch (5 cm) juveniles are frequently found alone in shallow, sheltered areas grazing on coral polyps. Adult specimens will reach a maximum length of about 7 inches (18 cm). The juveniles colouration is very similar to the adult except the white outline of the black lateral spot disappears as the fish increases in size.
This butterflyfish has also been observed off the East African coast, Madagascar, the Seychelles, Mauritius, Indonesia, Philippines, Marshall Islands, and Tahiti.
It is very rarely imported and extremely difficult to maintain in an aquarium.

13.
Chaetodon bennetti
Sub-adult, 2.9 in. (7.5 cm), aquarium photo. One should refrain from keeping this beautiful fish in an aquarium, due to the difficulty in providing an adequate food for this species, which feeds exclusively on coral polyps.

14.
Chaetodon bennetti
Adult, 6 in. (15 cm), underwater photo from the Great Barrier Reef.

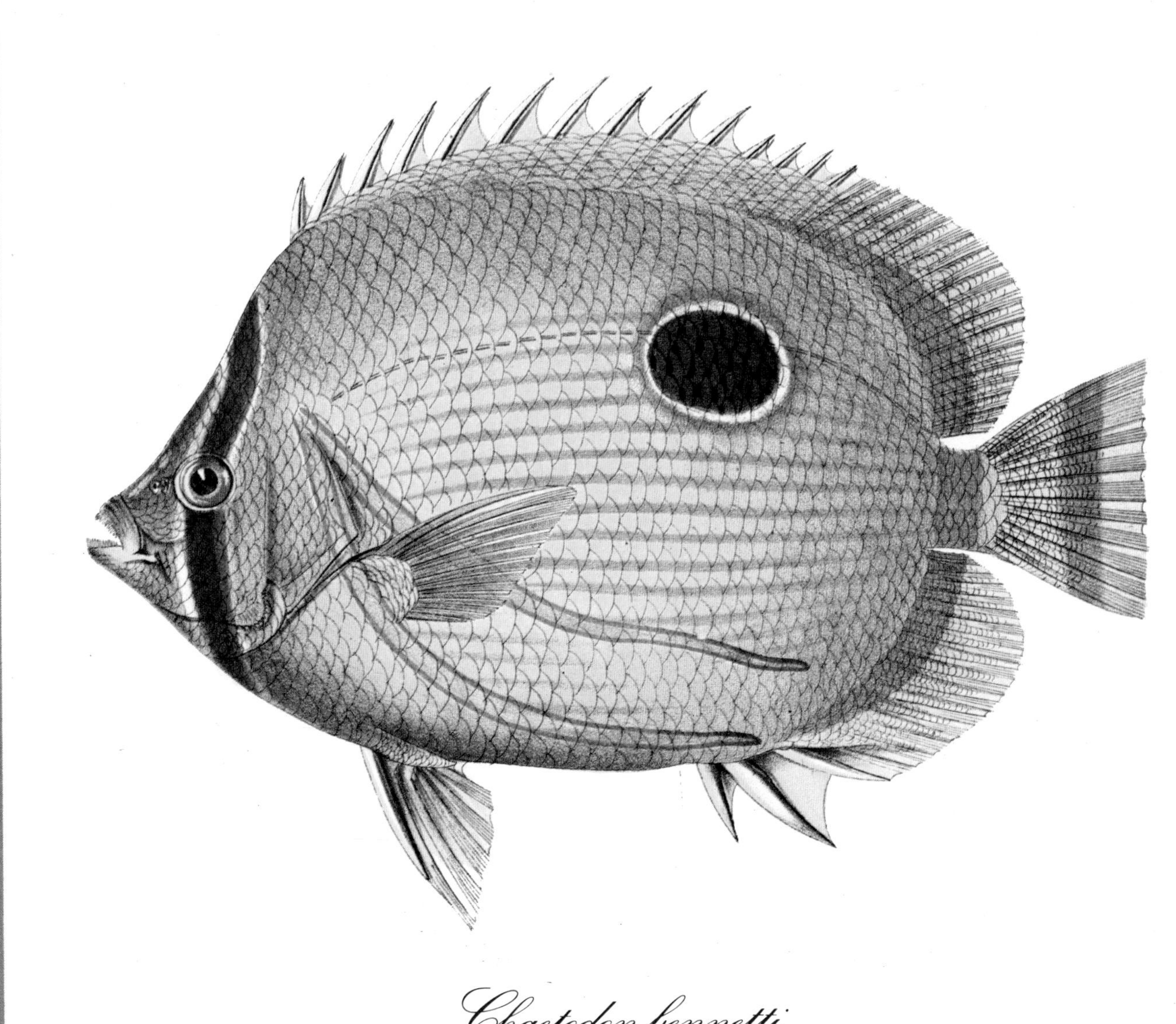

Chaetodon bennetti

Chaetodon citrinellus CUVIER, 1831
Speckled Butterflyfish

15 ▲ 16 ▼

This species is common on the Great Barrier Reef and New Guinea, inhabiting both the inner and outer reefs, often being the most common butterflyfish in areas of sparse coral growth. Apart from the afore-mentioned regions, the Speckled Butterflyfish has been recorded from the coastal waters of New South Wales and Western Australia and is also widespread in the Western Pacific, where it prefers depths of 1–10 metres (3-33 ft.). An aggressive species, which frequently erects the dorsal spines and faces downwards in a defensive position when approached by other fishes or a diver. The basic body colour varies from bright yellow to extremely light yellow or whitish. *C. citrinellus* retains the same colour pattern throughout its development and reaches a length of 5 inches (12.5 cm). Its diet consists of coral polyps, algae, and polychaetes.

15.
Chaetodon citrinellus
4.75 in. (12 cm), underwater photo.

16.
Chaetodon citrinellus
Adult,
4.75 in. (12 cm), aquarium photo.

Chaetodon ephippium CUVIER, 1831
Saddled Butterflyfish

Growing to a length of nine inches (23 cm), this species is widespread in New Guinea and is also found in New South Wales and Western Australia. In addition, the Saddled Butterflyfish has been recorded from the Indian Ocean as far as the East African coast and from the Pacific Ocean as far northward as Japan and Hawaii and southward to Tahiti. It is common in depths less than 10 metres (33 ft.) in areas of extensive coral growth. Pairs are frequently encountered and ripe females are easily distinguished during the breeding season because of their distended abdomen. The colour and markings undergo only a slight change from the juvenile to adult stage as illustrated. The diet is composed mainly of coral polyps, algae, shrimp, and polychaetes.

17.
Chaetodon ephippum
Juvenile specimen, 1.25 in. (3 cm), underwater photo.

Care and maintenance of *C. ephippium* in a tank is extremely difficult as most of the time it will refuse to eat.

18.
Chaetodon ephippum
Adult specimen, 8 in. (20 cm), underwater photo from the Great Barrier Reef.

17 ▲ 18 ▼

Chaetodon flavirostris GÜNTHER, 1873

Black Butterflyfish

A common species on the Great Barrier Reef, the coast of southern Queensland and New South Wales, including Lord Howe Island. According to RANDALL the geographic range includes the South Pacific as far as Pitcairn Island. It is found in a variety of habitats ranging from rich coral growth to algae covered rocks. On the Great Barrier Reef adult pairs with a length of 8 inches (20.5 cm) are commonly seen on the outer reef, while juveniles prefer the protected inner reefs. The behaviour of this species differs according to locality. They are generally timid on the Great Barrier Reef but are easy to approach and occur in large schools at Lord Howe Island. Food requirements in captivity are similar to those of *C. aureofasciatus*, page 14. Maintaining the Black Butterflyfish is difficult.

21. *Chaetodon flavirostris* Adult, 6 in. (15 cm), underwater photo.

20. *Chaetodon flavirostris* Adult, underwater photo.

19. *Chaetodon flavirostris* Juvenile, 2 in. (5 cm).

19 ▲ 20 ▼

Chaetodon güntheri AHL, 1913

Günther's Butterflyfish

Growing to a length of 6 inches (15 cm), this is a sub-tropical species found at Lord Howe Island and New South Wales at depths between 5 and 30 metres (16 and 100 ft.). Scattered individuals are observed at Lord Howe Island mostly outside the lagoon in areas of rich coral growth. AHL originally recorded this species from the Indo-Malaysian region, but on the basis of recent expeditions to the area its occurrence there is doubtful. It is possible that the original specimen was mis-labeled or perhaps it is confined to deep water in the Indo-Malayan region and therefore seldom seen. The species is also known from Japan. The colouration of this butterflyfish is similar to *C. miliaris* and *C. assarius.*

22. *Chaetodon güntheri* Adult 5 in. (12.5 cm).

22 ▼

Chaetodon kleinii BLOCH, 1790
Klein's Butterflyfish

One of the smaller members of the family which rarely grows to more than 5 inches (12.5 cm). It is common in New Guinea and Queensland and extends as far south as the Sydney area. It also occurs in the Indian Ocean as far as the East African coast, and in the Pacific Ocean as far as the Marshall Islands in the north and Tahiti in the south.

Usually this species is found on reefs that have a sandy coral bottom and little surge. There is very little colour change with growth except as the fish matures the mark above the eye becomes bright blue almost to the point of being luminous. Although one of the delicate members of the family, this species is rather hardy after it adapts to tank life.

23 ▲

24 ▲

26 ▼

25 ▼

23.–25.
Chaetodon kleinii
Juveniles of different sizes: 2 in. (5 cm) and 3.4 in. (8.5 cm).

26.
Chaetodon kleinii
Sub-adult, 3.4 in. (8.5 cm), aquarium photo. All kinds of food obtainable on the market are accepted, living Artemia and frozen food, however, are preferred.

Chaetodon lineolatus Lined Butterflyfish

CUVIER, 1831

A giant among the butterflyfishes, *Chaetodon lineolatus* reaches a length of 12 inches (30.5 cm). Native habitat: New Guinea, east coast of Australia as far as Sydney. It has also been recorded from Western Australia and is widespread in the Indian and Western Pacific Oceans, including Hawaii. Not an extremely common variety, this species is often seen feeding on coral polyps on inner reefs. Adult specimens are shy and thus difficult to approach at close quarters. In an aquarium, the Lined Butterflyfish will accept a wide variety of foods.

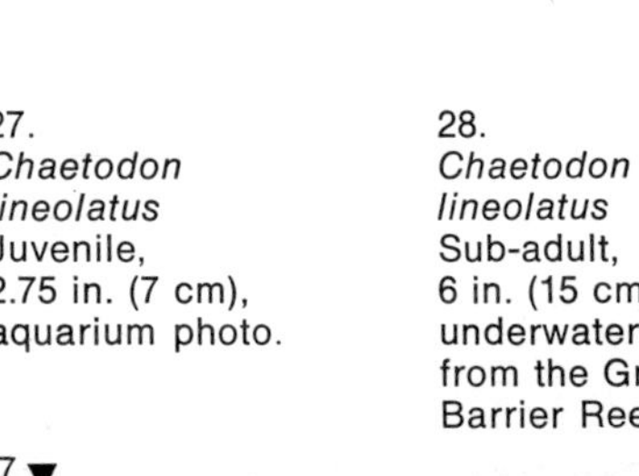

27. *Chaetodon lineolatus* Juvenile, 2.75 in. (7 cm), aquarium photo.

28. *Chaetodon lineolatus* Sub-adult, 6 in. (15 cm), underwater photo from the Great Barrier Reef.

27 ▼

28 ▶

Chaetodon lunula (LACÉPÈDE, 1803)
Racoon Butterflyfish

29 ▲ 30 ▼

This is one of the most popular chaetodontids differing rather dramatically in pattern from the juvenile to the adult stage. Attaining a length of 8 inches (20.5 cm), the Racoon Butterflyfish is very timid, and is usually seen alone, in pairs, or in schools of up to 20 individuals on inner reefs. The depth range is usually between 1–5 metres (3–16 ft.). They range throughout New Guinea and tropical Australia as far south as northern New South Wales. However, the species is not common in this region. It has been recorded from numerous Indo-Pacific localities, with the exception of the Red Sea, as far as Hawaii.
HIATT and STRASBURG (1960) reported that *C. lunula* feeds exclusively on coral polyps in the Marshall Islands.

29.
Chaetodon lunula
Juvenile,
1.5 in. (4 cm),
underwater photo.

30.
Chaetodon lunula
Adult, 7 in. (18 cm),
underwater photo.

C. lunula adapts easily to tank life and can be maintained without difficulty although it is sensitive to nitrate and nitrite as all butterflies are. Feeding the Racoon Butterflyfish is no problem: it should be offered deep-frozen Artemia, flake food, and freeze-dried red mosquito larvae.

Chaetodon lunula

Chaetodon melannotus BLOCH and SCHNEIDER, 1801

Black-backed Butterflyfish

This striking species can change colour dramatically if frightened or when observed at night. The dorsal portion of the body turns black except for two white patches, hence the common name. However, this colour phase is rarely seen under normal conditions. Found throughout the Great Barrier Reef, New Guinea and New South Wales. It also occurs across the Indo-Pacific from the coast of Eastern Africa as far as the Fiji Islands, mostly in shallow water, lagoons, or pools.
The Black-backed Butterflyfish is quite unafraid, and pairs are commonly observed usually in the vicinity of conspecific individuals. Reaching a maximum of 6 inches (15 cm), the species is well-suited for aquarium life and is easily maintained.

31 ▲ 32 ▶

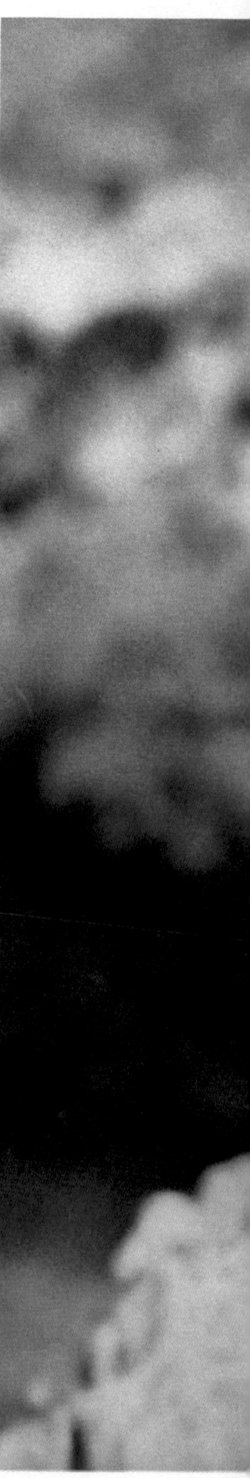

33 ▲ 34 ▼

31.
Chaetodon melannotus
Juvenile,
1,5 in. (38 mm), underwater photo from the Red Sea.

32.
Chaetodon melannotus
Adult, 5 in. (12.5 cm), underwater photo from the Great Barrier Reef.

33.
Chaetodon melannotus
Adult, underwater photo from the Great Barrier Reef.

34.
Chaetodon melannotus
Adult, in night-time or fright colouration.

Chaetodon melannotus on the Reef

Chaetodon mertensii CUVIER, 1831
Merten's Butterflyfish

Closely related to *Chaetodon xanthurus* from the Philippine Islands, Merten's Butterflyfish is usually found in deep water from 15–20 metres (50–66 ft.) adjacent to drop-offs. Juveniles are seen in groups, while the adults are mostly solitary, only occasionally occurring in pairs. The maximum size attained is about 5 inches (12.5 cm). Merten's Butterflyfish is very timid and seldom seen. It is found on the Great Barrier Reef and at New Guinea, but also ranges as far east as the Tuamotu Islands and as far west as the African coast. *C. paucifasciatus,* which is similar in appearance, occurs in the Red Sea. The three species in this complex are well-suited for tank life, preferring a vegetable diet.

Compare with: *Chaetodon paucifasciatus* AHL and *Chaetodon xanthurus* BLEEKER
These two species will be described in detail in volume 2.

35. *Chaetodon mertensii*
Adult, 4 in. (10 cm), underwater photo from the Great Barrier Reef.

36.
The colour pattern of *Chaetodon paucifasciatus* closely resembles that of *Chaetodon mertensii.* The former sub-species abounds in the Red Sea only. The specimen from our aquarium photo is 3.5 in. (9 cm) in size.

37.
Chaetodon xanthurus
A fish species which is known from the Philippines. After a period of adaptation it often proves to be sturdy aquarium fish.

◄ 35 36 ▲ 37 ▼

Chaetodon meyeri BLOCH and SCHNEIDER, 1801
Meyer's Butterflyfish

The first recorded specimen of *Chaetodon meyeri* in Australia is the fish illustrated here. Is was photographed in 1973 on the outside of Flynn Reef off Cairns, Queensland, in 10 metres (33 ft.) depth. The habitat consisted of thick coral growth. It was easily approached and browsed on coral polyps while being observed. This species has also been recorded from Heron Island, Queensland and Exmouth, Western Australia, as well as vast areas of the Indo-Pacific, extending from the East African coast to Hawaii. The juvenile pattern is simliar to that of small *ornatissimus,* except that the latter species has a gold marking instead of black. As the fish reaches maturity the fine markings on the face and dorsal area disappear. Reaching a maximum size of about 8 inches (20.5 cm), this butterflyfish has seldom been imported. Its maintenance in an aquarium is extremely difficult as it feeds exclusively on coral polyps.

38 ▲ 39 ▼

38.
Chaetodon meyeri
Juvenile,
1.75 in. (4.5 cm),
aquarium photo.

39.
Chaetodon meyeri
Adult, 6 in. (15 cm),
underwater photo
from the Great
Barrier Reef.

Chaetodon octofasciatus BLOCH, 1787
Eight-banded Butterflyfish

40 ▲ 41 ▼

A common species in New Guinea, inhabiting shallow protected areas at depths to 15 metres (50 ft.). Not yet observed in Australia, it has also been recorded from widespread locations in the Indo-Pacific from the East African coast and the Seychelles to the Fiji Islands. The species grows to five inches (12.5 cm) and is generally seen in pairs or small aggregations grazing on coral or algae. Juvenile specimens have the same markings as the adults and can be found alone or in small groups sheltering among heavy stands of coral. This butterflyfish is not a popular aquarium fish because in nature it feeds exclusively on coral polyps. It can learn to take artemia (brine shrimp) in captivity.

40.
Chaetodon octofasciatus
Juvenile, 2 in. (5 cm), aquarium photo. The yellow colouration of the adults appears after the fish has reached a size of approximately 3 in. (8 cm).

41.
Chaetodon octofasciatus
An adult pair of this striking species of approximately 4 in. (10 cm) length. Underwater photo from New Guinea.

Chaetodon ornatissimus CUVIER, 1831
Ornate Butterflyfish

As the name implies, the Ornate Butterflyfish is one of the most beautiful members of the family. It is largely restricted to outer reefs, at least throughout the Queensland and New Guinea portion of its range. It has also been recorded from various localities in the Western Pacific, including Hawaii. The preferred habitat includes areas of moderate surge to depths of 15 metres (50 ft.). It is generally a shy species. Juveniles are seldom seen and the adults are only encountered in small numbers. Individuals are sometimes observed in New Guinea swimming in company with the closely allied *C. meyeri.* The maximum length attained is about 7 inches (18 cm). The maintenance of this species in a tank is extremely difficult. Most of the time imports do not live more than eight weeks, probably because of their failure to adapt to aquarium food. In their natural environment they feed exclusively on coral polyps.

42 ▲ 43 ▼

42. *Chaetodon ornatissimus* Juvenile specimen, 1.75 in. (4.5 cm). The colour of the longitudinal bars is much darker than in the adults.

These fish require lots of space as in their natural surroundings they live a nomadic existence.

43. *Chaetodon ornatissimus* Adult specimen, 7 in. (18 cm), underwater photo.

Chaetodon pelewensis Dot-and-Dash Butterflyfish

KNER, 1868

This species is abundant on the Great Barrier Reef, particularly off Lizard Island, North Queensland, where it is found on outer reefs at depths of 1–30 metres (3–100 ft.). It is closely related to *C. punctatofasciatus* and it is not uncommon to see the two swimming in mixed pairs, particularly in the northern sectors of the Great Barrier Reef. The species has also been observed at Rabaul and in northern areas of New South Wales. Growing to 5 inches (12.5 cm), *C. pelewensis* is a shy fish, and is frequently observed feeding on coral. The pattern of transverse bars on the dorsal portion of the body is variable. This fish adapts itself easily to tank life and willingly accepts nearly all kinds of food offered.

44. *Chaetodon pelewensis* Adult specimen, 4 in. (10 cm), underwater photo from the coastal waters of New Guinea.

44. ▼

Chaetodon plebeius CUVIER, 1831

Blue-spot Butterflyfish

Widespread over the entire Great Barrier Reef and also found at Western Australia and New Guinea, *Chaetodon plebeius* is a ubiquitous species which seldom exceeds five inches (12.5 cm) in length. It is found in a variety of environments including coastal reefs to a depth of 10 metres (33 ft.). These small mouth chatodontids have been observed cleaning external parasites from other fishes in captivity. The adults frequently occur in pairs and are easily captured, but are susceptible to shock under stress conditions. Individuals are sometimes stranded in coral pools during low tides. In an aquarium, these fish should be offered live foods only, such as brine shrimp.

45 ▲ 46 ▼

45.
Chaetodon plebeius
Juvenile specimen with the blue dorsal marking still missing, 2 in. (5 cm), aquarium photo. The Blue-spot Butterflyfish has special requirements with regard to aquarium water quality: The fish should be offered an algae-grown tank, free of nitrate, which will help to prolong its life-span.

46.
Chaetodon plebeius
Adult specimen, 4 in. (10 cm), underwater photo from the Great Barrier Reef. This species grows to about 5 in. (13 cm). It has been recorded from coral seas all over the world, except the Caribbean.

Chaetodon punctatofasciatus CUVIER, 1831
Spot-banded Butterflyfish

This species is closely related to *C. pelewensis* and the two are frequently found together. It attains the same size as *C. pelewensis* and is found at similar depths. The habitat of *C. punctatofasciatus* includes the China Sea, extending from Japan to Taiwan. It has also been recorded from the Philippines and the Indonesian-Australian area as far as the Great Barrier Reef. The Spot-banded Butterflyfish is exported to Europe and the USA from the Philippines. Its maintenance in an aquarium is not difficult as this species accepts all kinds of food, even flake varieties.

47.◀
Chaetodon punctatofasciatus
Adult specimen, 3.5 in. (9 cm), underwater photo from the Great Barrier Reef. This species is relatively easy to maintain in a tank. Unfortunately, it is rarely exported to Europe.

Chaetodon punctatofasciatus x pelewensis Hybrid

In the northern areas of the Great Barrier Reef and at New Britain, individuals are occasionally encountered that have neither the exact markings of *C. punctatofasciatus* nor *C. pelewensis,* but are obviously close relatives. It is possible that these individuals represent hybrids between the two.

48. *Chaetodon punctatofasciatus x Chaetodon pelewensis?* The underwater photo shows a specimen of 4 in. (10 cm) in length.

49. *Chaetodon punctatofasciatus* Adult 3 in. (8 cm), aquarium photo.

48 ▲

49 ▼

Chaetodon rafflesi BENNETT, 1830
Latticed Butterflyfish

This large-scaled member of the family is very common around Rabaul and also occurs on the Great Barrier Reef, but is not abundant there. It also ranges widely in the Western Pacific as far as Tahiti. The Latticed Butterflyfish grows to a length of 6 inches (15 cm) and is often encountered in protected areas or inner reefs between 1 and 10 metres (3 and 30 ft.) depth. The distinctive colour pattern consists of a yellow ground with darker scale margins resulting in a latticed effect, giving the fish its common name.
Occasionally, this species is exported from the Philippine Islands to the USA. In a tank, these finicky eaters should be offered algae stones as well as so-called "feeding-stones", which are prepared by spreading the food pulp over the stone, and small crustaceans.

50 ▲ 51 ▼

50.
Chaetodon rafflesi
Sub-adult specimen,
2.5 in. (6.5 cm),
aquarium photo.

51.
Chaetodon rafflesi
Adult specimen,
5.5 in. (14 cm),
underwater photo.

Chaetodon rainfordi McCULLOCH, 1923
Rainford's Butterflyfish

Restricted to the Great Barrier Reef, adjacent coastal areas, and Lord Howe Island, this species grows to a length of 6 inches (15 cm) and is found at depths from 1 to 10 metres (3 to 33 ft.) either singly or in pairs. It is unafraid and easily approached.
C. rainfordi dwells in areas of sparse coral growth and feeds largely on algae. As far as the author knows, only a few specimens have been imported to the USA. Apparently it has never been exported to Europe. Its maintenance is possible only in an aquarium with heavy algae growth. The food requirements are similar to those of *C. aureofasciatus:* enchytrae and fully-grown artemia are preferred.

52.
Chaetodon rainfordi
Adult, 5 in. (12.5 cm), underwater photo.

53.
Chaetodon rainfordi
Juvenile, approximately 1.25 in. (3 cm), aquarium photo.

54.
Chaetodon rainfordi
3 in. (7.5 cm), aquarium photo.

52 ▲

53 ▼

54 ▼

Chaetodon reticulatus Reticulated Butterflyfish

CUVIER, 1831

A seldom seen species which inhabits the outermost slopes of the Great Barrier Reef in depths from 2–30 metres (6–100 ft.). In addition, *C. reticulatus* ranges widely in the Pacific Ocean, as far as Hawaii. It is frequently encountered in the coastal areas of Tahiti. Unlike many of the butterflyfishes, this species is easily approached by a diver. Small groups have been observed on deep isolated reefs and areas of rich coral growth. The bright, red-orange spot at the base of the soft anal fin is not present in juveniles but appears at maturity. The fish attains a maximum length of about 6 inches (15 cm). Exports from Hawaii to the USA are infrequent and the Reticulated Butterflyfish has come to Europe only on rare occasions. It is a species for the connoisseur only, as maintenance in a tank is difficult because of feeding problems. Live food of all kinds and a large algae-grown tank are recommended when keeping this fish.

55.
Chaetodon reticulatus
Adult specimen, 5 in. (12.5 cm), underwater photo.

56.
Chaetodon reticulatus
Adult, underwater photo from the Great Barrier Reef. This species closely resembles *Chaetodon collare* from the Indian Ocean and Red Sea, a frequently imported fish which is relatively easy to keep by an experienced aquarist (see volume 2).

55 ▼ 56 ▶

Chaetodon reticulatus on the Reef

Chaetodon selene BLEEKER, 1853

Yellow-dotted Butterflyfish

A poorly known species which has been recorded from West New Guinea. *C. selene* was not observed by the author in spite of several field trips to the Papua-New Guinea region. It is included here on the basis of records which appear in scientific literature. In the Moluccas it occurs in coral reef areas to depths of at least 20 metres (66 ft.). The photo is of a specimen from Ambon, Indonesia, taken by Dr. Gerald Allen. The drawing has been taken from Bleekers "Atlas of Indo-Malayan Fishes". There are no records available dealing with the care and maintenance of this butterflyfish in an aquarium.

57.▲
Chaetodon selene
Adult, 4 in. (10 cm).

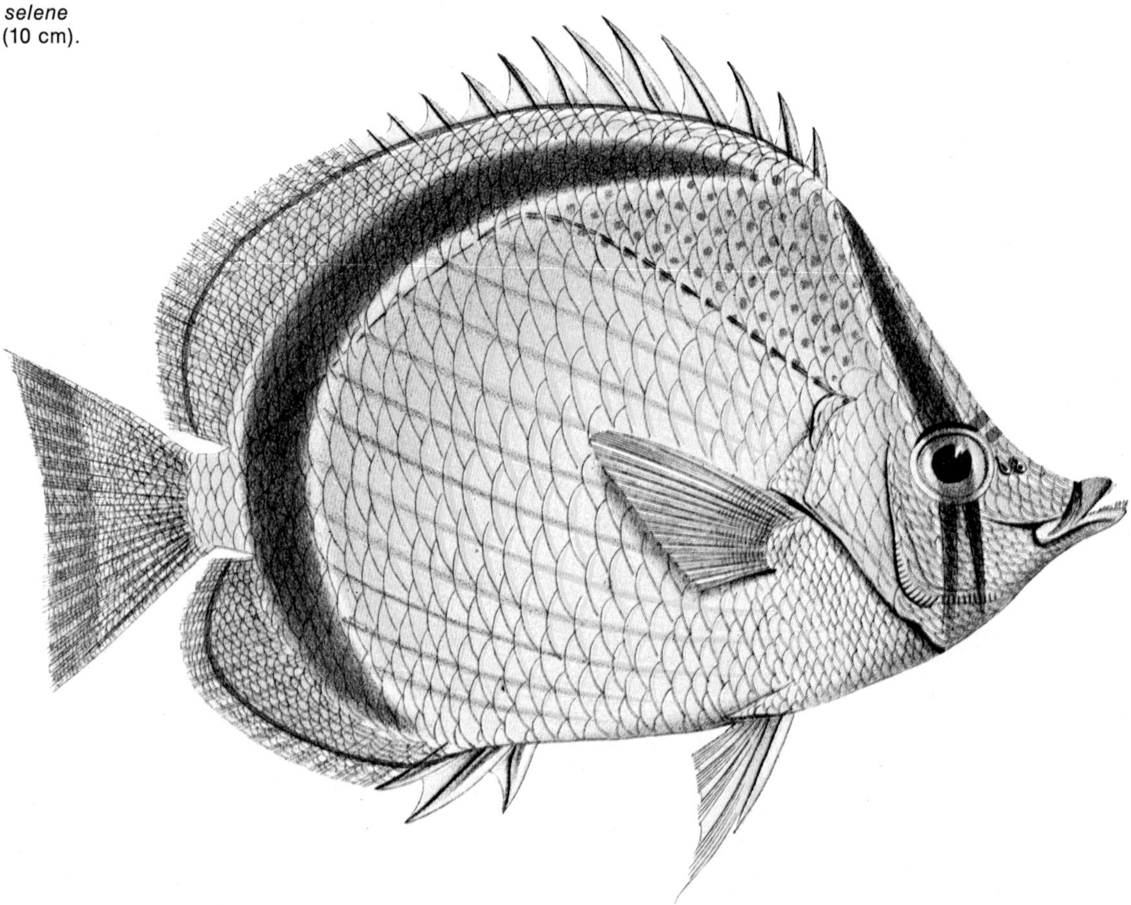

Chaetodon semeion BLEEKER, 1855
Dotted Butterflyfish

Another seldom seen species which inhabits the Great Barrier Reef and the New Guinea region. Adults 10 inches (25.5 cm) long were observed near Rabaul, New Britain. The species ranges widely in the eastern Indian Ocean and Western Pacific from Sri Lanka (where it is rare) to Tonga and the Marshall Islands. The filamentous extension of the soft dorsal rays is a distinctive feature shared also by *C. auriga* and *C. ephippium.* As the fish increases in size, the black stripe running through the eye becomes reduced until there is only a grey patch above the orbits. The abdominal region of females is noticeably thick set. The Dotted Butterflyfish is seldom exported to the USA and Europe.

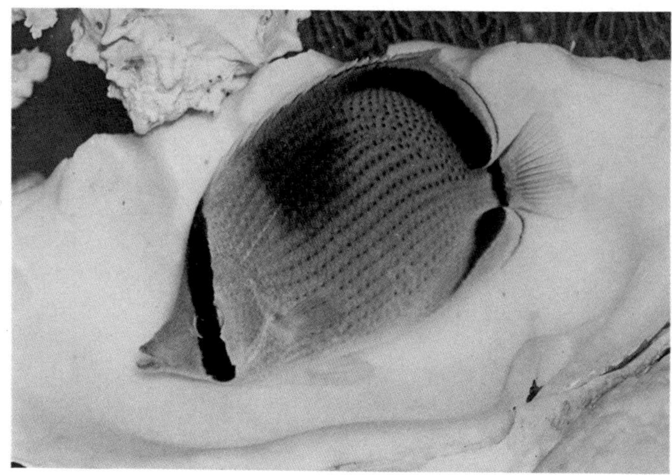

58.▲
Chaetodon semeion
Sub-adult, 4.75 in. (12 cm), aquarium photo.

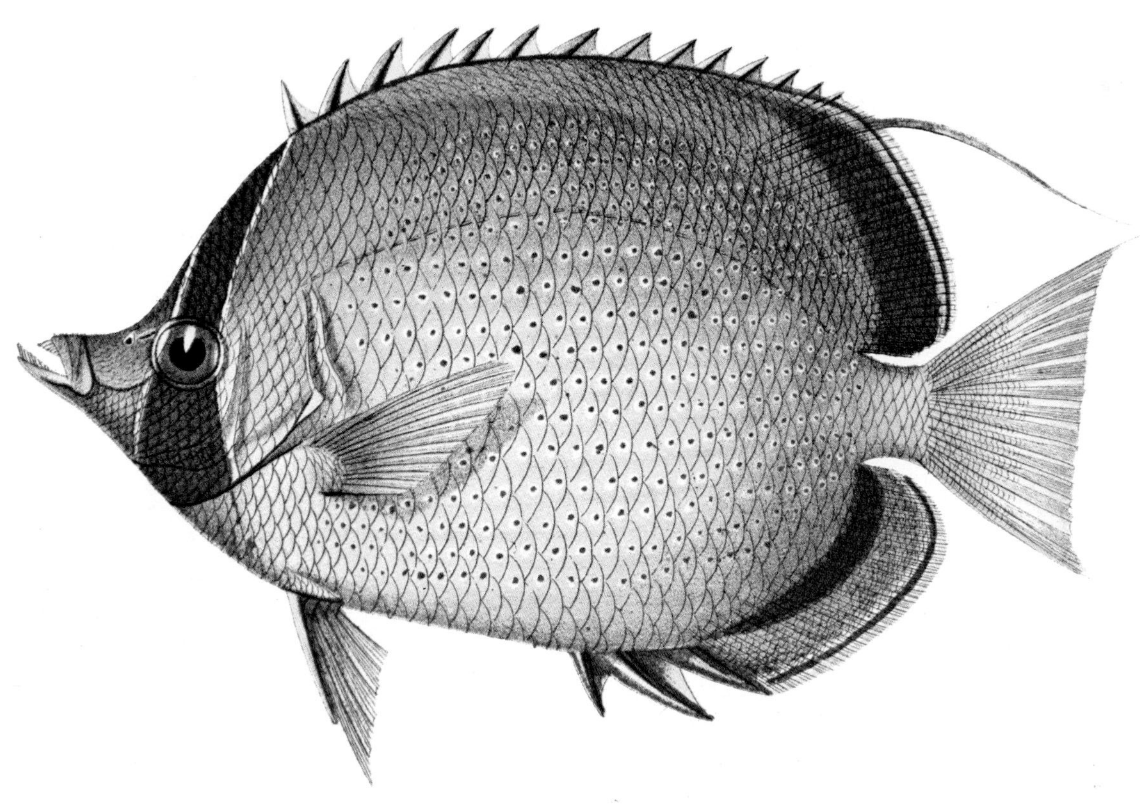

Chaetodon speculum Oval-spot Butterflyfish

CUVIER, 1831

A common fish in the northern extremities of the Great Barrier Reef, this species is also found in New Guinea and Western Australia. Outside this area the distribution encompasses the far Western Pacific from Indonesia to Japan. It reaches a length of 6 inches (15 cm) and retains the basic juvenile colouration when mature. It generally occurs singly and can be found in lagoons in one metre (3 ft.) of water as well as on outer reefs to a depth of 10 metres (33 ft.). It is a shy fish that nearly always retreats to shelter when approached. The Oval-spot Butterflyfish closely resembles *C. unimaculatus;* its colouration, however, is of a more intense yellow and lacks the black band, running from the dorsal to the anal fin (see illustration on page 51). Occasionally, *C. speculum* has been exported to the USA from the Philippine Islands. Although a rare guest in European tanks, it is said to be a sturdy fish which readily adapts to tank life. It has the same food requirements as *C. kleinii.*

59.
Chaetodon speculum
Sub-adult,
2.75 in. (7 cm),
aquarium photo.

60.
Chaetodon speculum
Sub-adult,
3 in. (8 cm),
underwater photo.

59 ▼

60 ▶

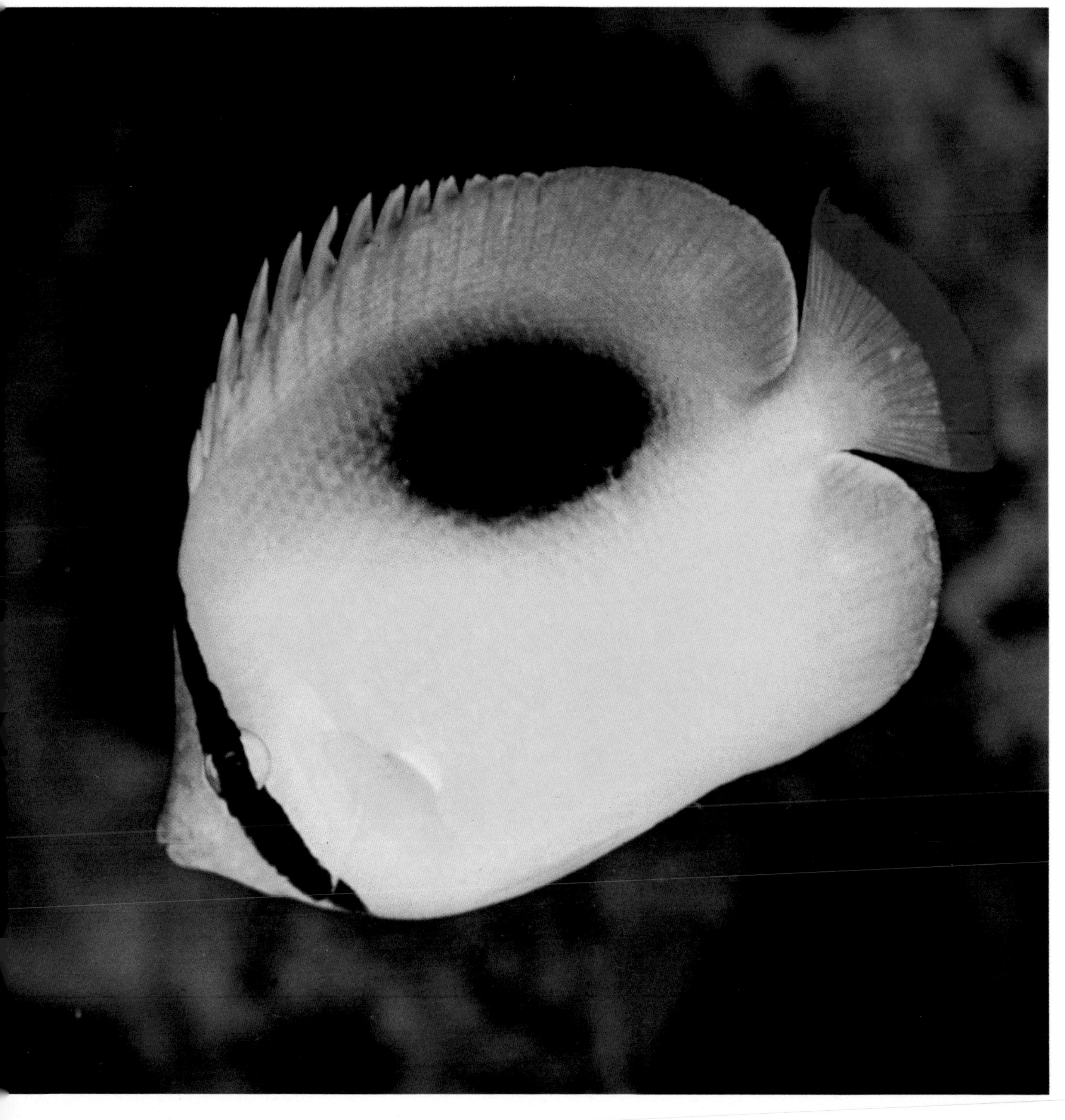

Chaetodon tricinctus WAITE, 1901
Three-stripe Butterflyfish

This species is found at Lord Howe and Norfolk Islands. At the former locality it is the most abundant Chaetodon in the lagoon, in areas of rich coral growth. Individuals are also observed outside the lagoon to a depth of 10 metres (33 ft.). The species generally occurs in small aggregations or in pairs. A maximum size of 7 inches (18 cm) is attained and juveniles and adults have the same basic colouration.
The Three-stripe Butterflyfish, as is true of all fish inhabiting the Great Barrier Reef, has only rarely been imported and is therefore relatively unknown to American and European aquarists. Information from Australian hobbyists regarding this species would therefore be greatly appreciated.

61 ▼

61.
Chaetodon tricinctus
Adult, approximately 6 in. (15 cm), underwater photo.

Photos on page 47:

62.
Chaetodon trifascialis
Juvenile specimen with a black bar at the end of the body and a yellow caudal fin; approximately 1.5 in. (3.8 cm).

63.
Juvenile specimen, 2.9 in. (7.5 cm). The caudal fin begins to change its colour.

64.
Sub-adult; approximately 4 in. (10 cm).

65.
Adult specimen; showing the typical colour pattern when frightened or observed at night.

Chaetodon trifascialis QUOY and GAIMARD, 1824
Chevroned Butterflyfish

This species was formerly referred to as *Megaprotodon strigangulus.* Adults attain a length of 7 inches (18 cm) and differ from the young by having a pointed dorsal fin and lacking the large black posterior band. It is widespread over the Great Barrier Reef and New Guinea and has also been recorded from Western Australia and the entire Indo-Pacific from the Red Sea to Hawaii. The normal depth range is between 2 and 5 metres (6 and 16 ft.). According to a study by Dr. E. S. REESE, which appeared in the scientific journal "Copeia", this species establishes territories over large plate-like heads of *Acropora* coral. Both males and females hold separate territories, although they are sometimes adjacent. Recent experiments by EHRLICH, TALBOT, RUSSELL, and ANDERSON, on the Great Barrier Reef, using plywood models of chaetodontids to test responses of various butterflyfishes, have indicated that this species exhibits the strongest reaction to intruders. One individual attacked a model of *C. auriga* so violently that scales became detached from the attacking fish.
At night, or when frightened, this species is able to change colours most effectively. Maintaining the Chevroned Butterflyfish successfully in a tank is almost impossible, as it feeds almost exclusively on coral polyps, i. e. *Acropora.* Nevertheless, this very common species is frequently imported.

62 ▲

63 ▼

65 ▼

64 ▼

Chaetodon trifasciatus PARK, 1797
Red-fin Butterflyfish

66 ▲

67 ▼

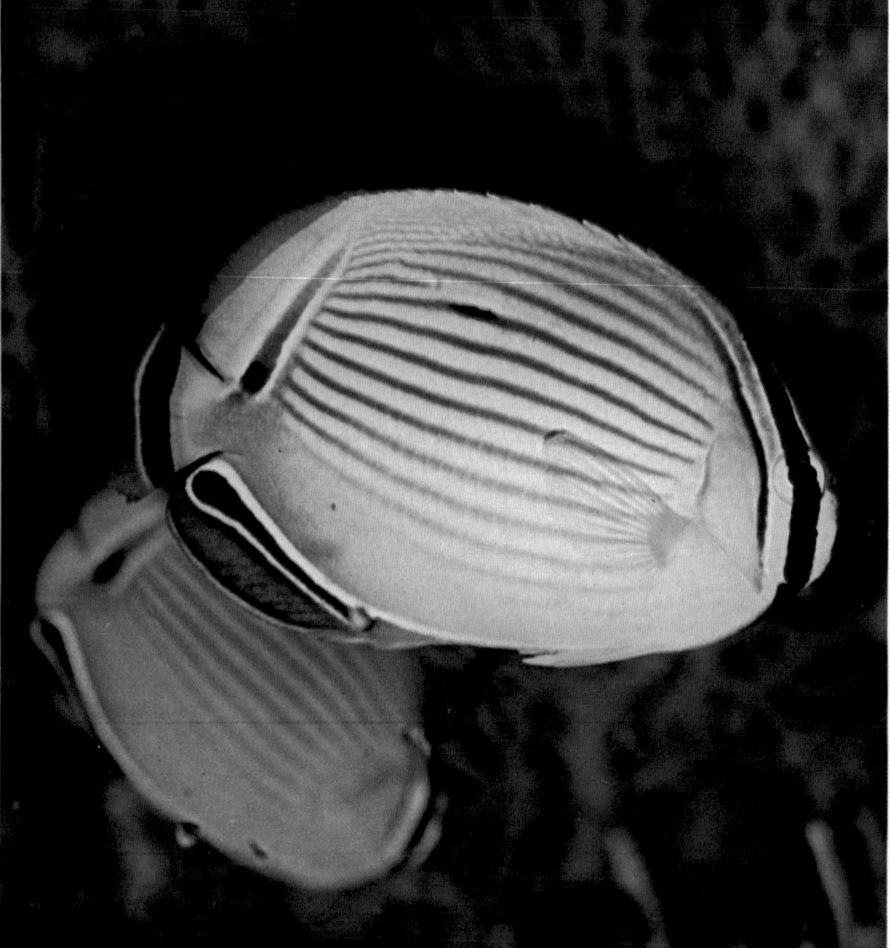

66.
Chaetodon trifasciatus
Juvenile specimen, 2 in. (5 cm), with a tear-drop like ocellus at the caudal peduncle. Aquarium photo.

67.
Chaetodon trifasciatus
Adult pair from the Great Barrier Reef. Size 5 in. (12.5 cm), underwater photo.

A common species which inhabits protected coral reefs of Queensland, Western Australia, and New Guinea. The Red-fin Butterflyfish is widespread over the entire Indo-Pacific. Sub-species or closely related species have been encountered in the Red Sea and the Arabian Gulf, and around Mauritius (see volume 2). They are a shallow dwelling fish that are frequently seen feeding on coral polyps. It has been suggested that male and female specimens of this fish can be told apart by the colour of the spiny part of the anal fin which appears pink in females and red in males. The species attains a mature size of 5 to 6 inches (12.5 to 15 cm). Dr. E. S. REESE reported that *C. trifasciatus* characteristically occured in pairs and unlike some butterflyfishes, it did not establish territories but roamed widely over the reef apparently avoiding other species especially other conspecific pairs.

Keeping this species successfully in a tank is extremely difficult, as it feeds exclusively on coral polyps in its natural environment. Some juveniles will willingly accept mysis, artemia, and tubifex in an aquarium. Their willingness to accept such food probably depends on the region where they were caught and on their condition after long transport. Aquarists should therefore buy only specimens of less than 4 inches (10 cm), and should be sure the fish accepts food in the dealer's tank.

68.
An aquarium photo of the brilliantly coloured *C. trifasciatus*, one of the most beautiful among the butterflyfishes.

BURGESS recognized this colour variation with the yellow caudal peduncle as a subspecies: *C. trifasciatus trifasciatus*.

Chaetodon ulietensis CUVIER, 1831
Pacific Double-saddle Butterflyfish

69 ▲ 70 ▼

Formerly known as *C. falcula,* a closely related species which is confined to the Indian Ocean, *C. ulietensis* is not a common species but is encountered throughout Queensland, Northwestern Australia, and New Guinea. It is widespread in the Western Pacific and tends to be more common around Tahiti and the Fiji Islands where it is encountered in large schools; normally it occurs singly or in pairs at depths between 5 and 10 metres (16 and 33 ft.). The preferred habitat is coraliferous areas where currents are frequently pronounced. Attains an adult size of 6 inches (15 cm). In contrast to *C. falcula,* this butterflyfish is not frequently exported. The hobbyist will soon find out that this is quite a voracious species, accepting nearly any kind of food. Consequently, this fish should be easily maintained in a tank.

For comparison: *C. falcula*
Indian Ocean
Double-saddle Butterflyfish

The difference is easily seen by comparing the markings of the anal fin and the form of the dark saddles.

69.
Chaetodon ulietensis
Juvenile,
1.5 in. (3.8 cm),
underwater photo.

70.
Chaetodon ulietensis
Adult,
5 in. (12.5 cm),
underwater photo from the Great Barrier Reef.

71. ▼

71.
For comparison:
Chaetodon falcula
Sub-adult,
4 in. (10 cm). This species has never been observed in Australian waters.

Chaetodon unimaculatus BLOCH, 1787
Teardrop Butterflyfish

A beautifully coloured fish, the adult grows to a length of 9 inches (23 cm). Unusually large specimens exhibit a "deformed" mouth which is shown in the photograph. Often found in groups of three or more, the species is generally not common and is timid. It frequents depths between 1 and 15 metres (3 and 45 ft.) in areas of prolific coral growth. The geographic range of this species includes the entire Indo-Pacific, extending from the Red Sea to Hawaii. It has also been recorded from New Guinea and Queensland as well as the north coast of New South Wales. Dr. E. S. REESE reported that stomach contents of this species contained large fragments of stony and soft corals and also sponge spicules, filamentous algae, and polychaete remains.

72 ▲ 73 ▼

72.
Chaetodon unimaculatus
Juvenile specimen, 3.5 in. (9 cm), aquarium photo. The tear-drop like spot can still be clearly seen; the lower part of it fades in adult specimens.

73.
Chaetodon unimaculatus
Adult, 8 in. (20 cm). This photo was taken in the Green Island Aquarium. Smaller species of less than 4 in. (10 cm) are easily maintained in a tank, as they willingly accept any kind of food offered by the aquarist.

Chaetodon vagabundus LINNAEUS, 1758
Vagabond Butterflyfish

This is one of the most common species in the Indo-Pacific, including Queensland and New Guinea. The Vagabond has been recorded from the coast of New South Wales south to Sydney. Attaining a length of 7 inches (18 cm), this fish is found in aggregations, pairs, or alone in a variety of habitats, including coastal reef exposed to freshwater run-off. They sometimes swim high off the bottom and are quite unafraid and easily approached. If harrassed by a diver, they tend to hold their ground rather than retreat to shelter. The diet consists mainly of coral polyps and algae. Nevertheless, there are usually no feeding problems in captivity if kept in water of an excellent quality which is frequently changed. After a period of time this species will become tame and accept flake food from its owner's hand.

The Vagabond is really *the* Butterflyfish for the beginner, but the aquarist must bear in mind that even the most easy to keep butterflyfish is at least as difficult to keep as a freshwater discus.

C. decussatus, a closely related species, will appear in volume 2.

74. *Chaetodon vagabundus* Juvenile, 1 in. (2.5 cm). In the posterior part of the dorsal fin the ocellus can clearly be seen. Underwater photo.

75. *Chaetodon vagabundus* Juvenile, 2 in. (5 cm), aquarium photo.

76. *Chaetodon vagabundus* Adult specimen, 6 in. (15 cm), underwater photo.

74 ▲ 75 ▼ 76 ▶

Chaetodon sp.

Chaetodon sp. (Picture no. 77)
Cape Butterflyfish
This individual was recently collected off Northwest Cape, Western Australia. The juvenile shown here exhibits certain colour pattern characteristics of *Chaetodon auriga* and *C. lunula.* It possibly represents a hybrid between these two species. The fish in question is 3.5 inches (9 cm) in length.

Rafflesi Hybrid
(Pictures no. 78 and 79)
Cairns Butterflyfish
This species was collected in April 1975 on the Great Barrier Reef off Cairns. The colour and general markings indicate an affinity to *C. rafflesi, C. pelewensis* and *C. vagabundus.* It possibly represents another hybrid. The specimen, below left, is approximately 1.5 inches (4 cm) in size; when photographed it had been maintained in a tank for a period of 6 months. The illustration, below right, shows the same fish at a length of approximately 2.5 inches (6 cm).

77 ▲

78 ▼

79 ▼

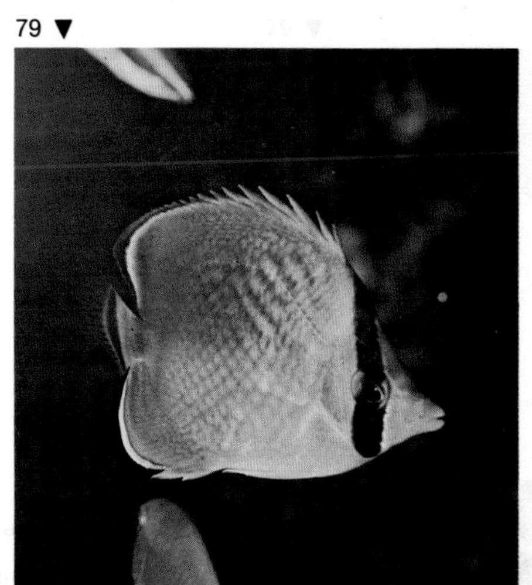

Green Island on the Barrier Reef

Aerial photo of the underwater observatory and island which has an interesting public aquarium.

◄ 80

Genus
Chelmon

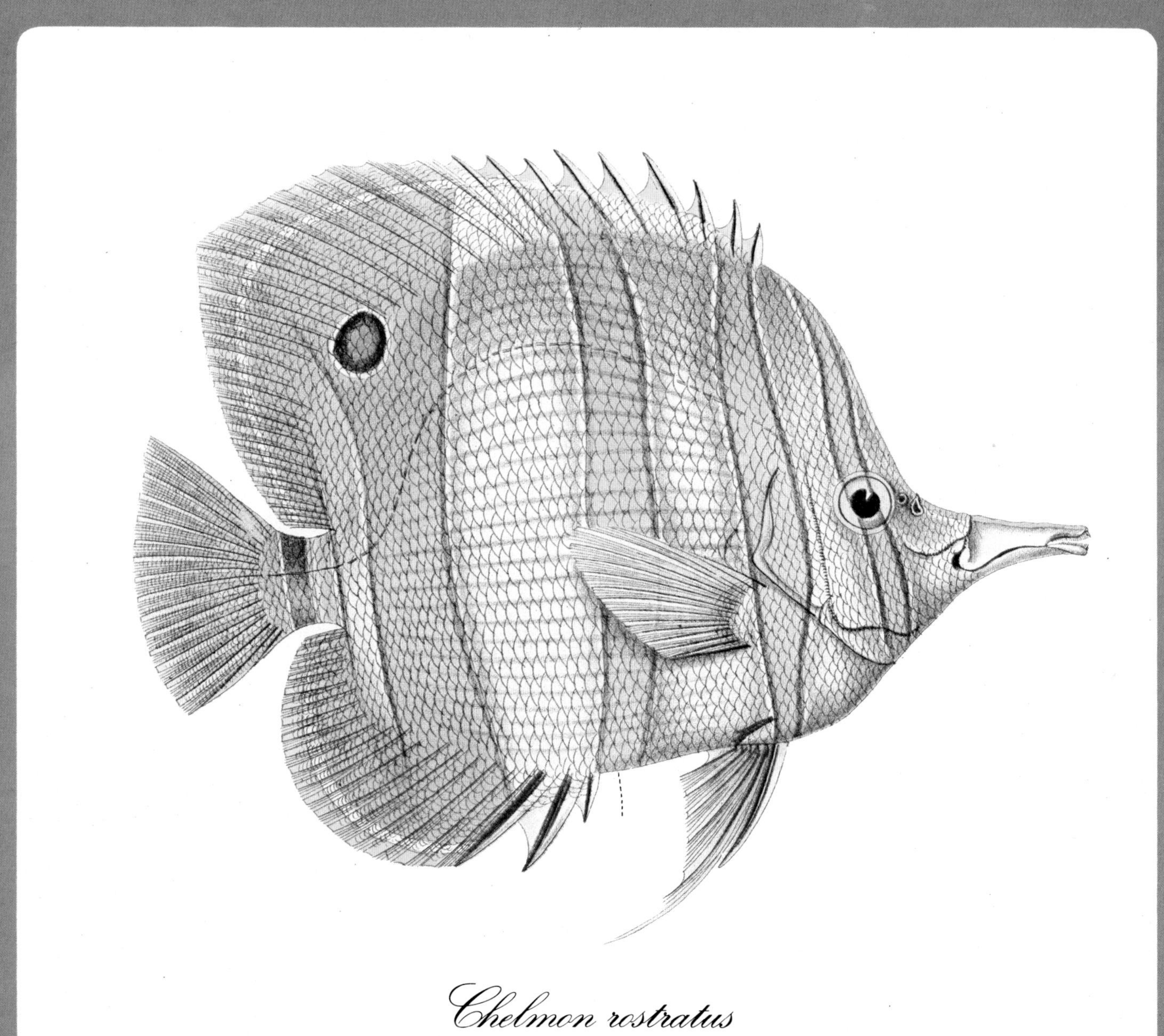

Chelmon rostratus

Chelmon marginalis RICHARDSON, 1842
Margined Coralfish

This species closely resembles *C. rostratus* (page 58) but adults lack the mid-body bar of that species, in addition to other colour differences. It is recorded from Western Australia, Northern Territory, and from the Home Group northwards on the Great Barrier Reef. The species occurs singly or in pairs at depths from one to 30 metres (3 to 100 ft.). The Margined Coralfish has probably never been kept in North-American or European tanks. The care and maintenance would resemble that of *C. rostratus* as the two species are closely related.

◄ 81

Chelmon mülleri (KLUNZINGER, 1879)
Müller's Coralfish

Found exclusively on coastal reefs and estuaries of Queensland, this species, unlike most other butterflyfishes, prefers algae covered and mud bottom areas instead of live coral reefs. A maximum size of 8 inches (20.5 cm) is attained and adults usually occur in pairs. They are a close relative of *C. rostratus* and these two species often co-occur in the same areas. The snout is noticeably shorter than in *C. rostratus* and as the fish matures a prominent protuberance develops on the nape. Unfortunately there are no aquarium data at hand, either from North American or from European hobbyists. The fact, however, that Müller's Coralfish co-occurs with *C. rostratus* indicates they may have similar aquarium requirements.

82 ▲ 83 ▼

82.
Chelmon mülleri
Juvenile,
1.4 in. (3.5 cm),
underwater photo.

83.
Chelmon mülleri
Adult, 6 in. (15 cm),
underwater photo.

Chelmon rostratus (LINNAEUS, 1758)
Beaked Coralfish, Copper-banded Butterflyfish

The Beaked Coralfish exhibits the elongated snout which, along with other characteristics such as 9 dorsal spines and 43–50 scales in a longitudinal series, set *Chelmon* apart from the genus *Chaetodon.* The elongated snout allows the fish to procure food items from hard to reach crevices in the coral reef. The Beaked Coralfish attains a length of 8 inches (20.5 cm), it frequents coastal areas and estuaries as well as coastal reefs. The species is recorded from New Guinea, Queensland, Northern Territory, and Western Australia. It also ranges widely in the Indian and Western Pacific Oceans. The usual depth range is one to 10 metres (3–33 ft.). The Beaked Coralfish is one of the most popular species for the saltwater aquarist. As this species likes to fight, so only one specimen should be kept in a tank. Frequent water changes are necessary for it to thrive. Feeding the Beaked Coralfish is sometimes difficult as they only accept live food, such as enchytrae, tubifex, and the tiny mysis; they might also take these foods if frozen fresh.

84 ▼

84.
Chelmon rostratus
Adult,
6.75 in. (17 cm),
underwater photo
from the
Great Barrier Reef.

85.
Chelmon rostratus
Juvenile,
1.25 in. (3 cm),
underwater photo.

▼ 85

Genus: *Chelmonops*

Chelmonops howensis (WAITE, 1903)
Lord Howe Coralfish

As the common name implies, this coralfish is found at Lord Howe Island, but it also occurs off the coast of northern New South Wales and southern Queensland. It is usually found in areas of live coral and is relatively easy to approach. The preferred depth generally ranges from 10–30 metres (33–100 ft.) and the species is seldom seen in shallow water. *Chelmonops* is distinguished from *Chaetodon* by having a different dorsal spine count, and a slightly different body shape. The maximum size is about 7 inches (17.5 cm). Current research may eventually result in the placement of this species into a different genus.

There are no data available concerning the fish's requirements in an aquarium. This coralfish has probably not yet been exported to the USA and Europe. BURGESS recently classified this species under *Amphichaetodon howensis.*

86. *Chelmonops howensis* This remarkable underwater photo of the Lord Howe Coralfish was taken at a depth of approximately 15 metres (50 ft.). The fish is 6 in. (15 cm) long.

86.▼

Chelmonops truncatus (KNER, 1859)
Talma

Growing to a length of 10 inches (25.5 cm), the Talma is a cool water species which is widespread across the southern half of Australia, appearing in southern Queensland, New South Wales, Victoria, South Australia and Western Australia. This fish usually occurs in pairs; they have been trawled down to 60 metres (200 ft.). The species feeds on algae and small invertebrates.
AHL describes this species as a "link" between *Chaetodon* and *Chelmon*. There are only a few records available regarding the tank life of the Talma, as is true for most of the Australian endemic fish.

87 ▲ 88 ▼

87.
Chelmonops truncatus
Juvenile,
1.5 in. (4 cm).
The ocellus is clearly visible.
Underwater photo.

88.
Chelmonops truncatus
Adult, 5.5 in. (14 cm), underwater photo from Western Australia.

61

Genus
Coradion

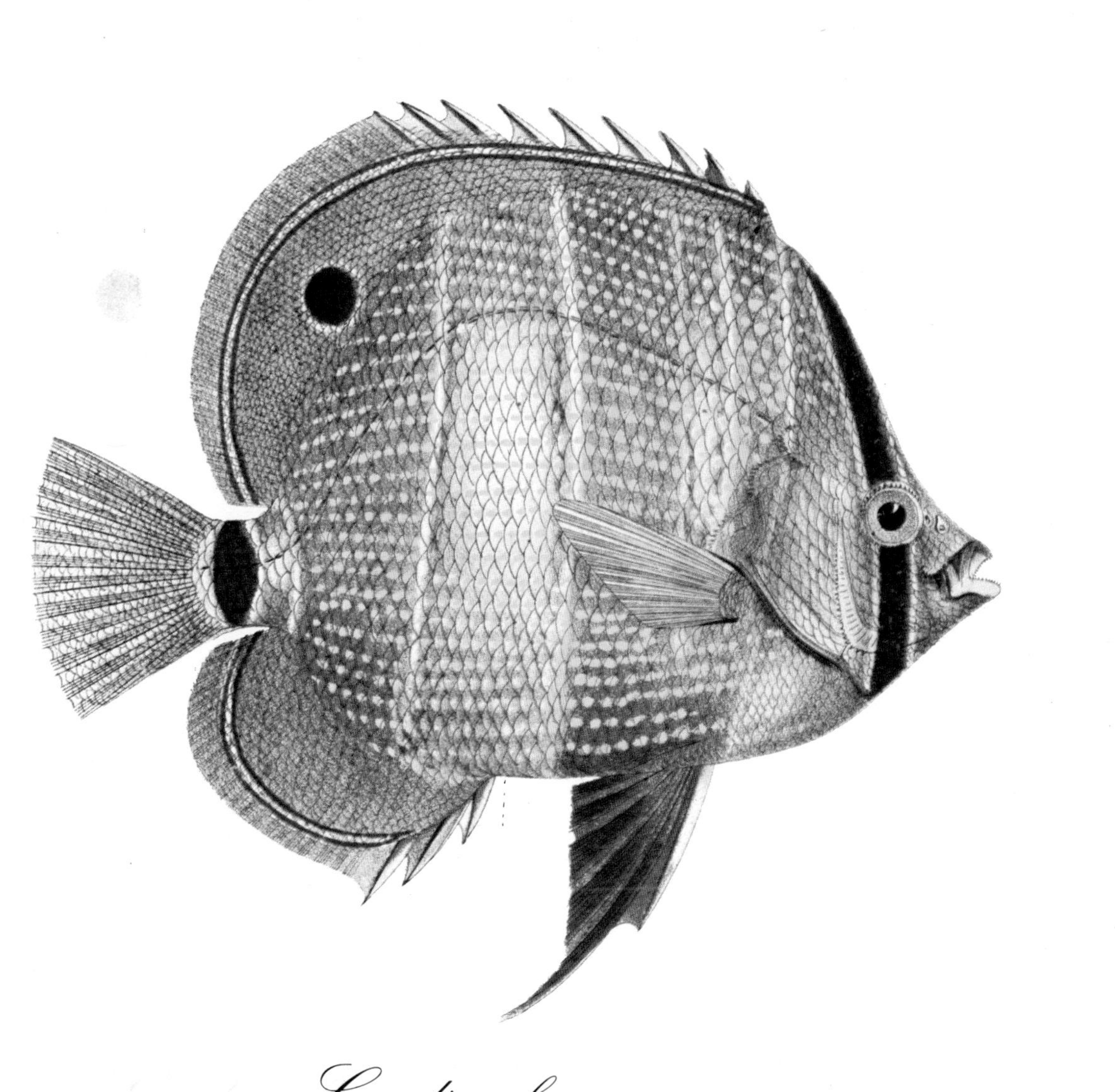

Coradion chrysozonus

Coradion altivelis McCULLOCH, 1916
Highfin Coralfish

One of the lesser known butterflyfishes, this species occurs sparingly in areas of live coral on the Queensland coast and around islands adjacent to the Great Barrier Reef, most noticeably around the Pompey, Swains, and Capricorn complexes.
According to AHL this species occurs from Sumatra to the east of New Guinea. It is often seen in these areas with *Coradion chrysozonus.* The maximum size reached is about 6 inches (15 cm). The genus *Coradion* differs from *Chaetodon* by having a lower dorsal spine count, usually 8—10 spines, compared with 11—15 spines. Unfortunately no aquarium data have been collected until now, as the Highfin has not been exported. Its demands and requirements in a tank, however, will most likely resemble those of the genus *Chelmon.*

89 ▼ 90 ▶

89.
Coradion altivelis
Juvenile,
1.25 in (3 cm),
underwater photo

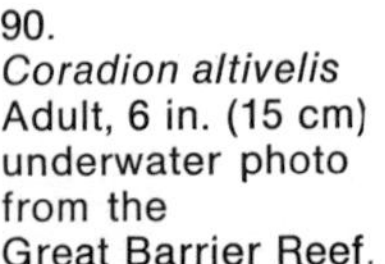

90.
Coradion altivelis
Adult, 6 in. (15 cm)
underwater photo
from the
Great Barrier Reef.

Coradion altivelis on the Reef

Coradion chrysozonus
Orange-banded Coralfish

This species is not common although it is found in scattered colonies along the Queensland coast, Western Australia, and New Guinea. It generally occurs in areas of sparse coral growth. Like *Parachaetodon ocellatus,* it is often brought up in trawl nets in Queenslands waters. The Frankland Group off north Queensland is one area in which this species abounds.

It has also been observed in the waters around Indonesia and the Philippines and – very seldom – along the Chinese coast. The maximum length attained is approximately 5 inches (13 cm). Sometimes, *C. chrysozonus* is offered as food-fish at the Manila fish market. There are no records regarding exports to Europe or the USA. It is possible that the Orange-banded Coralfish, like *Hemitaurichthys,* lives on a planktonic diet, thus enabling the hobbyist to keep it alive with a diet of live foods. See also illustration on page 61.

91. ▶ *Coradion chrysozonus* Adult, 6 in. (15 cm), underwater photo from the Great Barrier Reef.

(KUHL and VAN HASSELT in CUVIER, 1831)

Coradion melanopus (CUVIER, 1831)
Two-eyed Coralfish

92 ▲ 93 ▼

This species has not been recorded from Australia, but is present at New Guinea, ranging as far as the Moluccas. I observed it at Madang at a depth of 20 metres (66 ft.) in a sheltered lagoon with poor coral growth. At Rabaul, New Britain, it was sighted on an exposed outer reef in 30 metres (100 ft.). It grows to 6 inches in length (15 cm) and is an extremely wary fish. According to AHL, *C. melanopus* differs from *C. chrysozonus* by its less protruding lips and a longer snout. In addition, the Two-eyed Coralfish has a second spot on the anal fin which does not disappear in adult specimens. The grey-brown posterior body-bar has an orange-yellow border on both sides.

There is little data regarding the keeping and maintaining of the Two-eyed Coralfish in an aquarium.

92. *Coradion melanopus* Sub-adult, 3.5 in. (9 cm), aquarium photo.

93. *Coradion melanopus* Adult, 5 in. (12.5 cm), underwater photo. *C. melanopus* differs from the previous species by having an additional ocellus in the anal fin. The feeding of juveniles with brine shrimp and mysis is possible, some individuals even accept flake food. Frequent, small feedings are absolutely necessary for healthy growth of the juveniles.

Genus
Forcipiger

Forcipiger flavissimus

Forcipiger flavissimus JORDAN and McGREGOR, 1898
Long-nosed Butterflyfish

94 ▲

95 ▼

This species has a wider distribution than any other member of the family. It is found in the Red Sea and off the coast of Africa, and ranges across the Indo-Pacific to lower California and central America. It is common on the outer portion of the Great Barrier Reef and has also been recorded from Western Australia, New South Wales, and New Guinea. It is closely related to *F. longirostris* and these species are sometimes seen together. However, *F. flavissimus* is much more abundant throughout its range. Individuals are often seen browsing on live coral with their specially adapted snout. They are generally seen in depths between 1 and 30 metres (3 and 100 ft.) in areas of heavy coral growth. Generally, the Long-nosed Butterflyfish occurs singly or in small groups of up to five individuals. An all black colour phase was recently observed in Australian waters. Keeping this species in a tank is comparatively easy. After a period of adaptation, specimens in good condition will accept flake food from their owner's hand.

96 ▼

Forcipiger longirostris (BROUSSONET, 1782)
Big long-nosed Butterflyfish

94.
Forcipiger flavissimus
Adult, 5 in. (12.5 cm), underwater photo.

95.
Forcipiger flavissimus
4.75 in. (12 cm), aquarium photo.

96.
Forcipiger flavissimus
The illustration shows the shorter snout and the deeper mouth opening.

97.
Forcipiger longirostris
Adult, 7 in. (18 cm), underwater photo from the Great Barrier Reef.

This species resembles *F. flavissimus,* but can be visibly distinguished by its greater snout length. It also has 10–11 dorsal spines instead of the usual 12 exhibited by *F. flavissimus.* It is generally rare at Queensland and New Guinea; very few individuals have been sighted. It usually occurs alone or in pairs. An entirely black phase is sometimes seen on the Kona Coast of Hawaii (see volume 2).
The illustration shows *F. longirostris* in a classical threatening position among the coral gardens of the Great Barrier Reef. Because the Big long-nosed Butterflyfish is extremely rare, it has only been exported on a few occasions. It should be identically suited to aquarium life as *F. flavissimus.* Hawaiian aquarists have no problem keeping this species.

▼ 97

Genus: *Hemitaurichthys*

Hemitaurichthys polylepis (BLEEKER, 1857)
Pyramid Butterflyfish

This unusual and attractive fish has been seen in limited numbers off Australia and New Guinea. Barrier Reef localities, such as Raine Island, Escape Reef, and Jenny Louise Shoals, harbour small colonies. I have also seen the species on drop-off areas at Rabaul and it has been observed at the D'Entrecasteaux Group of New Guinea. It is also widespread over the Western Pacific, as far as Hawaii. Basically, it is a schooling fish, and the preferred depth range is between 5 and 25 metres (16 and 82 ft.) on offshore reefs. The diet probably consists largely of plankton. The maximum size reached is about 7 inches (18 cm). One character that separates this genus from most other members of the family is its smaller scale size (55–60 in a longitudinal row). It is not difficult to maintain this fish in a tank, which applies to most plankton feeding species.

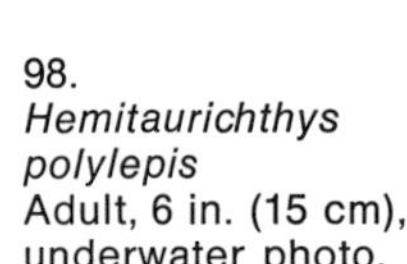

98.
Hemitaurichthys polylepis
Adult, 6 in. (15 cm), underwater photo.

98 ▲ 99 ▼ 100 ▶

99.
Aquarium photo of a specimen the same size as above. The black head colouration has faded away, which may indicate bad health. The bright colour may, however, also indicate that the fish is frightened.
It is best kept in a school of at least 3–5 specimens in a tank of not less than 300 litres (70 gallons) of water.
H. zoster, a related species, is found in the Indian Ocean only (this fish will be described in volume 2).

100.
A gorgeous school of *Hemitaurichthys polylepis* together with some *Chromis chrysurus* on the Great Barrier Reef. The dark head markings are clearly visible.

Genus
Heniochus

Heniochus acuminatus

Heniochus acuminatus (LINNAEUS, 1758)
Long-fin Bannerfish

There are six members of the genus *Heniochus* which inhabit the region covered by this book. This species is the most common and best known of the group.
It frequents coastal areas as well as offshore reefs and is sometimes seen in the vicinity of wharves. Growing to a length of 8 inches (20.5 ft.), it retains the basic juvenile colouration but the dorsal filament increases in length as the fish matures. The Long-fin Bannerfish occurs alone, in pairs or in small aggregations and is easy to approach. The elongated dorsal spines and the presence of bony protuberances on the forehead in some species are characteristics which distinguish this genus from other related butterflyfishes. Recorded from New South Wales, Queensland, Northern Territory, Western Australia and New Guinea as well as the entire Indo-Pacific over an area extending from the Red Sea as far as Hawaii.
The Long-fin Bannerfish is easily maintained in a tank. It is a good eater, accepting most foods, including the flake varieties. If, however, the food is refused, something might be wrong with the tank, or the fish may be in poor health. The recommended space allotment is at least 200 litres (50 gallons) for three fish of 6–8 inches (15–20 cm).

101.
Heniochus acuminatus
Fully-grown specimens, 7 in. (18 cm), underwater photo from the Great Barrier Reef.

▼ 101.

Heniochus chrysostomus CUVIER, 1831
Pennant Bannerfish

Previously known as *Heniochus permutatus,* this fish attains a length of 6 inches (15 cm). It usually inhabits areas of heavy coral growth at depths ranging from 1–15 metres (3–50 ft.). It is not as common as *H. acuminatus* and is often seen in company with *H. varius*, especially on the Great Barrier Reef. Juveniles can readily be found in shallow areas where they browse on coral and algae. Recorded from New Guinea, Western Australia, Queensland, and New South Wales. It is also widespread across the Western Pacific, ranging from the Indo-Australian Archipelago as far as Hawaii in the north, and the Tuamotu-Archipelago (north-east of Tahiti) in the south. The Pennant Bannerfish is a rare guest in home aquaria because it is rarely imported.

102.
Heniochus chrysostomus
Adult, 6 in. (15 cm), underwater photo.

103.
Heniochus chrysostomus
Sub-adult, 3 in. (8 cm), aquarium photo.

◄ 102 103 ▼

Heniochus diphreutes JORDAN, 1903
Schooling Bannerfish

This species is very similar to *H. acuminatus,* but differs by having an additional dorsal spine, and in the juvenile stage at least, it has a shorter snout and longer pelvic fins. In addition, the anal spines are white instead of black on Australian individuals and the species occurs in small to large mid-water groups. *H. acuminatus,* on the contrary, is generally solitary or occurs in pairs or small aggregations which are closely associated with the sub-stratum.

It attains a length of 8 inches (20.5 cm).
For many years, this species has been regarded as a mere variety of *H. acuminatus,* but a scientific paper currently in press by ALLEN and KUITER clearly defines the distinguishing characteristics of both species. Known from New South Wales, Western Australia, South Africa, Japan, the Hawaiian Islands, and the Red Sea.

104.
Heniochus diphreutes
Adult, 7 in. (18 cm), underwater photo.

104. ▼

Heniochus monoceros CUVIER, 1831

Masked Bannerfish

Retaining the basic colour pattern throughout its development, this species like some other members in the genus develops a characteristic protuberance on the nape. It attains a length of 9 inches (23 cm) and is found in areas of lush coral growth.
It is found over the entire Great Barrier Reef, and is also recorded from New South Wales and Rabaul, generally at depths to 20 metres (66 ft.).
In spite of its wide geographical range – from Mauritius to the Society Islands (Tahiti) – the Masked Bannerfish has not yet invaded the tanks of hobbyists. This may be due to the fact that this species grows to a larger size than other members of the genus and may not readily adapt to aquarium life.

105 ▲ 106 ▼

105.
Heniochus monoceros
Juvenile,
1.5 in. (4 cm),
underwater photo.

106.
Heniochus monoceros
Adult, 7 in. (18 cm),
underwater photo
from the
Barrier Reef.

Heniochus monoceros on the Reef

The smaller fish are *Lutjanus kasmira*

07

Heniochus singularius SMITH and RADCLIFFE, 1911
Singular Bannerfish

108 ▲ 109 ▼

This species is seldom seen in the Australian-New Guinea region. In New Guinea a few individuals were observed at Rabaul and Madang; in Australia one specimen has been recorded from Western Australia, while others have been observed at Stradbroke Island near Brisbane, and on scattered reefs of the Great Barrier Reef complex.
The Singular Bannerfish was discovered during the Albatross Expedition in the region of the Philippines; more recently it has been recorded from the waters around Indonesia, Malaysia, Formosa, and southern Japan. The favoured habitat consists of steep drop-offs in 10–40 metres (33–130 ft.) depth. A maximum size of 10 inches (25 cm) is reached at maturity.

108.
Heniochus singularius
Juvenile,
1.5 in. (4 cm),
aquarium photo.

There are no existing data regarding the tank life of this species. A few exports have been made from the Philippines for exhibit in large show tanks.

109.
Heniochus singularius
Adult, 8 in. (20 cm),
underwater photo
from Heron Island.

Heniochus varius (CUVIER, 1829)
Humphead Bannerfish

The common name of this species originates from the enlarged protuberance at the nape, and the horns that grow above the eyes of the adult. Growing to 7 inches (18 cm) length, this member of the genus is easily approached and observed. They have a preference for caves rather than open terrain, and are encountered mostly in pairs, although at Rabaul I observed a group containing about 30 individuals. The normal depth distribution is between 2—15 metres (6—50 ft.). The juvenile form does not have the forehead bump or horns and adults gradually lose the elongate dorsal filament of juveniles.

The species is widespread in the Western Pacific; in Australia it occurs in Queensland and Western Australia. It has been exported from the Philippines to the USA. In a tank, *H. varius* is more delicate than *H. acuminatus;* nevertheless, it can be successfully maintained if kept under the proper conditions. The food for young fish should be finely sieved. They should be fed *Artemia* 2—3 times daily. Adult brine shrimp which has the intestinal tract full of algae and pulverized vegetable matter, for example screened vegetable flake food, is an excellent food source which provides necessary vitamins. Juvenile Humphead Bannerfish are more interesting in appearance and it is therefore best to buy specimens not larger than 1.5—2.5 inches (4—6 cm) in size. Unfortunately, this species has rarely been exported to Europe.

Heniochus varius
Adult, 7 in. (18 cm), underwater photo.

▼ 110

Heniochus varius in the coral garden of the Reef

111 ▲ 112 ▼ 113 ▶

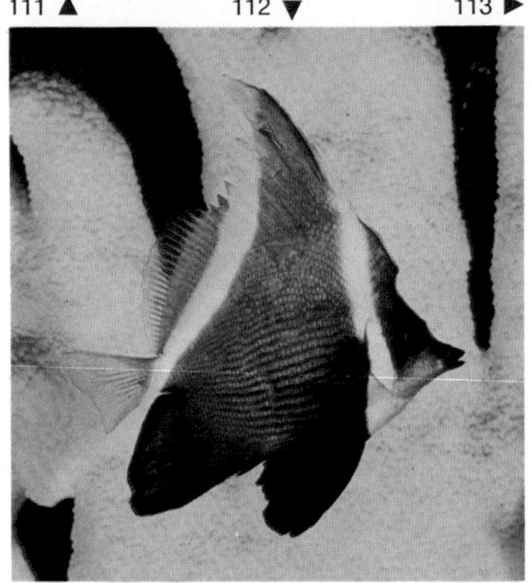

111./112.
Heniochus varius
Juveniles,
2 in. (5 cm) and
4 in. (10 cm).

113.
Juvenile,
2.5 in. (6 cm).
Underwater photo
from the
Barrier Reef.

Genus
Parachaetodon

Parachaetodon ocellatus

Parachaetodon ocellatus (CUVIER, 1831)
Ocellate Coralfish

114 ▲

115 ▲

116 ▼

This species is distinguished from other members of the family by a low dorsal spine count. Most butterflyfish and coralfish species have nine or more spines while *P. ocellatus* has only six. The distribution includes New South Wales, Queensland, Northern Territory, Western Australia, and West Irian New Guinea. It is also recorded from the eastern Indian Ocean, including coastal areas of India and Sri Lanka, and west to the Philippines, Indonesia, and southern China. It shows an affinity for coastal reefs, often in muddy areas. The maximum length is 7 inches (18 cm). Occasionally, the Ocellate Coralfish has been exported to the USA and Europe. Maintaining it in a tank is sometimes difficult.

114./115.
Parachaetodon ocellatus
Juvenile specimens, 1.5 in. (3.8 cm) and 2. in. (5 cm).

116.
A nearly full grown specimen, 4 in. (10 cm), aquarium photo.

117.
Parachaetodon ocellatus
Adult, 6 in. (15 cm), underwater photo.

▼ 117

Family: *Scorpididae* Halfmoons
Genus: *Atypichthys*

Atypichthys latus McCULLOCH and WAITE, 1916
Eastern Footballer

Both are common inshore species which inhabit rocky areas in 5 to at least 40 metres (16 to 130 ft.). They feed pre-dominantly on algae and attain a maximum length of about 7 inches (18 cm). The geographic range for *A. latus* includes the Kermadec Islands, New Zealand, Norfolk and Lord Howe Islands. The only significant characteristic by which *Atypichthys* can be differentiated from the following genus Microcanthus is the absence of vomerine teeth in the latter (according to FRASER-BRUNNER 1945). There are no data available concerning the keeping of *Atypichthys* in an aquarium. However, they probably have similar requirements to Microcanthus.

118. *Atypichthys latus*, Adult, 6 in. (15 cm).

Atypichthys strigatus (Günther, 1860)
Mado

118 a. *Atypichthys strigatus*
The species is recorded from New South Wales, southern Queensland, Western Australia, and Lord Howe Island.

118 a. ▲

118 ▼

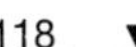

Genus: *Microcanthus*

Microcanthus strigatus (CUVIER, 1831)
Stripey

The Stripey (photos 119 and 120) is very common in rock pools along the southern coast of Queensland and at Lord Howe Island; it also inhabits coral reefs as far north as the Capricorn Group, Great Barrier Reef, and extends its range north from the Philippines as far as the southern coast of Japan, and is also encountered throughout the Hawaiian Islands, where it lives in shallow coastal waters (according to GOSELINE and BROCK).
A slightly different colour variation has been described separately as *M. vittatus.* It is exclusively confined to the coast of Western Australia, extending from the North West Cape south to Albany. However, this population probably represents a geographic variant of the wide ranging *M. strigatus.*

According to ALLEN, *M. strigatus* adapts easily to tank life and is especially suited for the novice.
It accepts a wide variety of foods including dry foods, algae, chopped beef, and small crustaceans. The requirements of the Stripey are similar to those of scats, which makes it a suitable addition for the aquarium.

119 ▲ 121 ▼ 120 ▶

119. *Microcanthus strigatus* Sub-adult, 4 in. (10 cm).

120. *Microcanthus strigatus* Adult, 5 in. (12.5 cm).

121. *M. (vittatus) strigatus* from Western Australia.

Genus: *Neatypus*

Neatypus obliquus

Western Footballer

WAITE, 1905

Another attractive member of the scorpidid family found only in the waters of Western Australia. These fish frequently travel in aggregations of up to fifty or more individuals. They are extremely tame and easy to approach at close range. The preferred habitat consists of areas of mixed rock and weed in depths between 6 and 30 metres (20 and 100 ft.).

The Western Footballer should be kept in schools in large tanks. However, this fish has not been introduced to North American or European hobbyists.

Neatypus obliquus
Adult, 6 in. (15 cm).
▼ 122

Genus: *Vinculum*

Vinculum sexfasciatum (RICHARDSON, 1842)
Moonlighter

Essentially a cool water fish, *Vinculum sexfasciatum* is found in Victoria, Tasmania, South Australia, and Western Australia. It is quite common on rocky reefs off the coast. On juvenile specimens there is a black ocellus on the anterior section of the soft dorsal and anal fins which disappears with age. Adults reach a maximum length of 10 inches (25.5 cm). *V. sexfasciatum* has been included in the *Chaetodontidae* by most previous authors (for instance AHL); it is, however, actually a member of the family *Scorpididae.* The Moonlighter has rarely been recorded as an aquarium fish. Keeping it in a warm water tank is not recommended, because of its low temperature demands (10–20° C). Thus far *V. sexfasciatum* has not been exported to North America and Europe. It is not likely to be introduced in the near future as there is virtually no commercial collecting activity along the southern coast of Australia.

The Moonlighter adapts readily to tank life if it does not suffer from transport damage. A shy and peaceful species, which should not be kept together with belligerent fish.
Food requirements: mysis.

▼ 123

Family
Scatophagidae

Scats

Scatophagus argus

Genus: *Scatophagus* Scats

For camparison:

Scatophagus argus (var. atro-maculatus) Mia-Mia or Spotted Scat (BENNETT, 1828)

Scatophagus argus (BLOCH, 1788) Common Scat

The family *Scatophagus* is related to the butterflyfishes but differs in several important respects: After hatching from the egg, larval butterflyfishes spend the first few weeks of life drifting in the open sea. During this period the young are silvery or transparent and the head is covered with bony plates. Young Scats are also pelagic for a short period but lack the bony armour which is a typical feature of the chaetodontid "tholichthys" larval stage. Scats inhabit estuaries, coastal harbours, and mangrove creeks. Adults attain a length of 12 inches (30.5 cm). The colour of mature individuals varies from silver to brown. The juveniles differ greatly in colour and were erroneously given a different name, *S. argus "rubrifrons"*, by fish importers. The Indian or Common Scat, shown here for comparison, has black circular spots all over the body. Any beginning saltwater aquarist should have at least one scat in his tank. Because of their voracious appetites, scats are often helpful for inducing the more delicate aquarium introductions to begin feeding.

124.
Scatophagus argus (var. atro-maculatus)
Juvenile form of the Australian variety. Unfortunately, they loose their beautiful red markings and stripes later on.

125.
Scatophagus argus
Juvenile,
1.5 in. (3.8 cm).
Has not been recorded from Australian waters.

126.
Scatophagus argus
Adult specimen.

127.
Scatophagus argus (var. atro-maculatus)
Adult,
10 in. (25.5 cm).
Australian specimen.

124 ▲

125 ▼

▼ 126

127 ▼

Genus: *Selenotoca*

Selenotoca multifasciata (RICHARDSON, 1844)
John Dory or Spot-banded Scat

Growing to 10 inches (25 cm), this species of Scat inhabits brackish estuaries and coastal waters. It also penetrates rivers and creeks of New Guinea, New Caledonia, northern Australia and New South Wales.
Aquarium maintenance is similar to that recommended for other members of the Scat family. It is necessary to handle all Scats with care as puncture wounds from the strong dorsal spines are painful.
In the southern part of Australia a similar species is found instead of *S. multifasciata,* which is known under the name of *Selenotoca multifasciata* (sub-species *aetate varians)* and which reaches a length of at least 15 inches (38 cm).

▲ 128

The different colour variations of Scats lead to confusion even today, as scientists cannot decide whether these colour changes represent different species or just variations:

		Native Habitat	Juvenile	Adult
Scatophagus argus BLOCH 1788 Common Scat Photo 126		Indonesia Philippines	with circular dots on the body. Photo 125	with circular dots on body and fins. Basic colour: green
Scatophagus argus *(var. atro-maculatus)* BENNET 1828 Mia-Mia or Spotted Scat Photo 127	Synonym: *Scatophagus ornatus,* trade name: *Scatophagus argus rubrifrons*	New Guinea, North and East Australia, Sri Lanka (Ceylon)	Red markings on the forehead. Black horizontal bars on the upper side of the body. Photo 124	Irregularly marked and dotted; basic colour green-silver with an occasional pink shimmer
Scatophagus argus *var. tetracanthus* LACÉPÈDE 1802 no illustration		Coastal waters of South Africa	4–6 bars, running from the upper to the underside of the body as well as on the pectoral and anal fins	6 broad vertical bars fading toward the lower part of the body from the middle

Family: *Enoplosidae* Old Wives
Genus: *Enoplosus*

Enoplosus armatus (WHITE, 1790)
Old Wife

This species is confined to the southern half of Australia. It is a schooling form which inhabits rocky areas. Large numbers are frequently seen among kelp beds. The maximum length is about 9 inches (23 cm). In an aquarium the Old Wife should be maintained at temperatures between 15–20° C. Feedings of brine shrimp, mysis, frozen food, and small worms are recommended. *E. armatus* has been occasionally exported to the USA.

129.
Enoplosus armatus
Juvenile,
2.5 in. (6 cm),
aquarium photo.

130.
Enoplosus armatus
Adult, 6 in. (15 cm),
aquarium photo.

129 ▲

130 ▼

Family
Pomacanthidae

Angelfishes

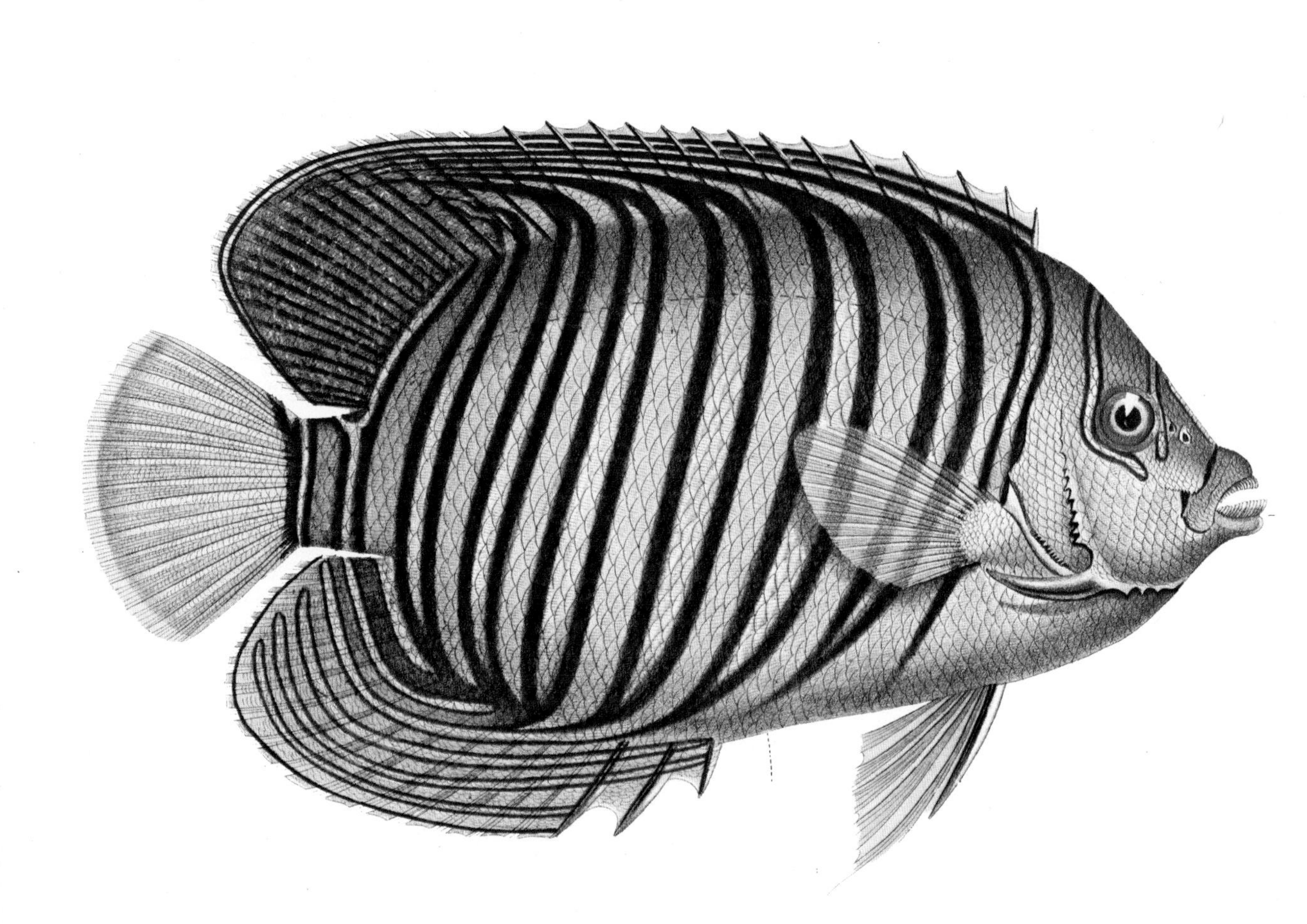

Pygoplites diacanthus

Genus: *Apolemichthys*

Apolemichthys trimaculatus (LACÉPÈDE ms., in CUVIER, 1831)
Three-spot Angelfish

131. *Apolemichthys trimaculatus* 5 in. (12.5 cm), aquarium photo.

131 ▲ 132 ▼

132. *Apolemichthys trimaculatus* Adult, 6 in. (15 cm).

This colourful species gets its common name from the two lateral spots and a third spot on the forehead. Many previous authors have placed it in the genus *Holacanthus,* but it is actually referrable to *Apolemichthys.* This genus is distinguished from other large angelfishes by having the preorbital bone convex and without strong spines. In addition, the large cheek spine lacks a deep groove and the dorsal and anal fins are rounded. The first individuals to be seen in Australia were observed 35 miles east of Cairns on a small coral reef outside the outer Barrier Reef. Three six-inch (15 cm) fish were encountered in a rich coral area at a depth of 15 metres (50 ft.). In addition, the species has been collected from Western Australia (Northwest Cape), Great Barrier Reef (Yonge Reef), and also inhabits outer reef areas of New Guinea. The Three-spot Angelfish is distributed throughout the Indo-Australian Archipelago, the Philippines, and in the Indian Ocean to the African coast (Zanzibar).

Maintaining this fish in a tank is possible, although there may be initial difficulties; the tank walls should be covered with algae and the hobbyist should offer mysis, artemia (frozen), flake food, freeze dried red mosquito larvae, and enchytrae. Special attention should be given to the water quality.

Genus
Centropyge

Centropyge tibicen

Centropyge aurantius Golden Angelfish

RANDALL and WASS, 1974

This species was recently described from several specimens collected at American Samoa. Three previously unreported specimens collected at Madang are deposited at the Australian Museum (Sydney). These were taken at a depth of 3–15 metres (10–50 ft.) among coral and sponges. Because of its cryptic habits this species is seldom seen; in late 1975 one specimen was collected at Carter Reef, Queensland. Aquarium maintenance of the Golden Angelfish is probably similar to other members of the family: Algae tank, vegetable diet, supplemented by tiny vertebrates. The specimen in the illustration is approximately 4 inches (10 cm) in length.

133 ▼

Centropyge bicolor (BLOCH, 1787)

Bicolor Angelfish

The genus *Centropyge* includes the smallest members of the family Pomacanthidae. *C. bicolor* is a common species at New Guinea and on the Great Barrier Reef. In addition, the geographic range includes the tropical Western Pacific from Indonesia, to southeast Polynesia (Tahiti etc.), but not including Hawaii. The preferred habitat of the Bicolor Angelfish consists of drop-offs and lush coral areas where it is usually seen in pairs or small aggregations. They are always encountered close to the bottom, in coral and rubble areas, and have the habit of quickly darting from one hiding place to the next. Juveniles can be found in water as shallow as 1 metre (3 ft.), but it is unusual to see adults in less than 10 metres (33 ft.).

134 ▲ 135 ▼

134.
Centropyge bicolor
Adult, 5 in. (12.5 cm), underwater photo.

135.
Centropyge bicolor
Sub-adult,
4 in. (10 cm),
aquarium photo.

Centropyge bicolor on the Reef

The same basic colouration is retained throughout the life cycle, however, in New Guinea the yellow colour is frequently more intense than on Australian individuals. Grows to 6 inches (15.5 cm) total length.
The Bicolor Angelfish is frequently imported, mostly from the Philippines. It is an easy fish for the experienced salt-water aquarist provided it is offered hiding places and an adequate diet which includes vegetable matter, small crustaceans, and worms.

136 a/b. ▶
These photos from the Moluccas show *Centropyge bicolor* singly and as a pair in their natural habitat.

Centropyge bispinosus (GÜNTHER, 1860)
Two-spined Angelfish

An extremely shy fish, *Centropyge bispinosus* is seldom seen away from cover and hence is difficult to photograph or collect. It is recorded from drop-offs of the Great Barrier Reef and those lying off the Madang area of New Guinea, but seldom in depths less than 5 metres (16 ft.). They usually occur singly or in small aggregations. The most southerly distribution recorded is Bass Point, south of Woollongong, New South Wales, where it was collected in early 1974. The geographic range of this angelfish includes South Africa, Mauritius, and the Seychelles in the Indian Ocean as well as Tahiti in the Western Pacific. The Philippines is another area in which this fish is abundant and from here it is exported all over the world. Specimens caught in the Philippines have a beautiful blue-red colouration (see illustration 137 and 138).

This fish is often erroneously called "C. kennedy" after the Philippine exporter Earl Kennedy.

137.
Centropyge bispinosus
Sub-adult,
2.75 in. (7 cm),
aquarium photo.

137 ▼

138.
Adult specimen with a gorgeous colouration. Aquarium photo.

139.
The typical colouration is responsible for the latin name. The fully-grown specimen in the illustration is a slightly unusual colour variant.

140.
Colour variant from the Great Barrier Reef, 2.6 in. (6.8 cm). Standard length.

141.
Adult specimen, 3 in. (8 cm). Colour variant lacking the usual stripes. Underwater photo.

142.
Adult specimen, 3 in. (8 cm). Typical colouration, showing the typical stripes. Underwater photo from the Great Barrier Reef.

Colour variations of Centropyge bispinosus

138 ▲ 139 ▼ 140 ▼ 141 ▲ 142 ▼

Centropyge eibli KLAUSEWITZ, 1963
Eibl's Angelfish

143 ▲ 144 ▼

This beautiful species was recently discovered at North West Cape, Western Australia, by Mr. John Braun. It was previously known only from the Maldive Islands where it was first collected by the German biologist Eibl-Eibesfeldt in 1963, for whom the species is named. It was also taken at Indonesia on a recent scientific expedition. It prefers rich coral areas in 10–20 metres (33–66 ft.) depth. One of the larger members of the genus, *C. eibli* reaches a maximum length of about 6 inches (15 cm).
Eibl's Angelfish is exported to the USA and Europe via Sri Lanka. Keeping it in a tank is comparatively easy, as it willingly accepts most foods which are offered.

143.
Centropyge eibli
Adult,
5.5 in. (14 cm),
aquarium photo.

144.
Centropyge eibli
Sub-adult,
4.25 in. (11 cm),
aquarium photo.

145.
Centropyge flavicauda
2 in. (5 cm),
aquarium photo.

146.
Centropyge flavicauda
Adult, 2 in. (5 cm).
Colour variation from the Southern Great Barrier Reef.

Centropyge flavicauda FRASER-BRUNNER, 1933
White-tail Angelfish

145 ▲ 146 ▼

147 ▼

The only Australian records of this species are from Spur Reef and Hick's Reef, North Queensland; Bass Point, Woollongong, New South Wales; and One Tree Island on the southern Great Barrier Reef. In New Guinea it is common at Madang over rubble bottom on the outer reef slope and on the edge of channels leading to the lagoon. The entire geographic range, however, is not sufficiently known. The normal depth distribution is between 10 and 20 metres (33–66 ft.), but in other parts of the Pacific it has been taken as deep as 40 metres (130 ft.). This is a small species, reaching only 2 inches in length (5 cm) at maturity. At first glance it is easily mistaken for a damselfish (family *Pomacentridae),* but the spine on the cheek is characteristic of angelfish, although difficult to see on live individuals as the species is extremely shy.
The aquarium maintenance of the White-tail Angelfish is similar to that recommended for other members of the genus *Centropyge.*
C. flavicauda is closely allied to *C. fisheri* from the Hawaiian Islands.

147.
For comparison: *Centropyge fisheri,* a closely related species with red and black pectoral markings.
Size 3 in. (8 cm), aquarium photo.

148.
Centropyge flavicauda
This underwater photo shows a specimen of 2.5 in. (6 cm), taken at Madang, New Guinea.

148 ▼

Centropyge flavissimus (CUVIER, 1831)
Lemonpeel Angelfish

149 ▲ 150 ▼

This species is the most common shallow water member of the genus in the islands of the Central Pacific. However, it is extremely rare in the Australian-New Guinea region. Throughout most of its range the Lemonpeel inhabits sheltered lagoon areas, but a specimen recently collected at One Tree Island in the Capricorn Group was captured in a surge channel on the outer reef in 3–4 metres (10–13 ft.). Juveniles have the same basic colouration as adults, except young males have a blue-rimmed black spot on their sides. Algae is the main dietary component.
Only under excellent water conditions, and in an algae-grown tank, will this angelfish survive. Apart from a vegetable diet, it will accept small crustaceans and worms.

Male juveniles have a black body mark on each side.

149. *Centropyge flavissimus*

150. *Centropyge flavissimus* Adult, 3.5 in. (9 cm).

Centropyge heraldi WOODS and SCHULTZ, 1953
Herald's Angelfish

This species is known from Australia on the basis of only a few specimens. One individual was living in an area of rich coral growth at Jenny Louise Shoals, Queensland, and was extremely timid. Herald's Angelfish has also been recorded at other Great Barrier Reef localities such as the reefs off Lizard and Lady Musgrave Island. The species is relatively widespread in the Central and Western Pacific. It is similar in appearance to *C. flavissimus* although it lacks the blue colouration around the eyes and gill covers. This species grows to a length of about 4 inches (10 cm). Aquarium maintenance is similar to that recommended for *C. flavissimus.* The lower picture shows two specimens on the reef; the other was photographed in a tank.

151 ▲

152 ▼

Centropyge loriculus (GÜNTHER, 1860)
Flame Angelfish

153 ▲ 154 ▼

This striking fish was first described from the Society Islands over a century ago. Because few individuals were sighted over the years it was all but forgotten until the 1960's when it was rediscovered at Johnston Island (southwest off Hawaii) in the Central Pacific. Unaware of GÜNTHER'S earlier description SCHULTZ mistakenly named the fish *C. flammeus*. The species is now known to occur in scattered localities in the Western Pacific including Egum Atoll off southeast New Guinea. The preferred habitat is the outer reef slope in 5–25 metres (16–82 ft.) depth. It is generally seen in areas of live coral. A size of about 4 inches (10 cm) is reached at maturity. This is perhaps the hardiest aquarium species in the genus and excellently suited for tank life. Because of its striking appearance, the Flame Angelfish is a valuable addition to every salt-water aquarium.

153. *Centropyge loriculus* Sub-adult, 2.75 in. (7 cm). Aquarium photo. This species is easy to keep in an aquarium.

154. *Centropyge loriculus* This striking red variety is an aquarium rarity that is much in demand. The illustration shows an adult specimen of 3.5 in. (9 cm) in length. Underwater photo.

Centropyge multifasciatus (SMITH and RADCLIFFE, 1911)
Multi-barred Angelfish

This species is slightly different in appearance than other members of the genus. It has 13 dorsal spines instead of the usual 14 or 15, and is more deep-bodied. The species is apparently widespread, but is seldom observed because of its deep dwelling habits. Only a few specimens have been seen at scattered localities throughout the Western Pacific. The only recorded observations from the region covered by this book were at the old sub-base near Rabaul, New Britain, where several individuals were seen in 20 metres (66 ft.) on a steep cliff face. In addition, it has been recorded from the Great Barrier Reef off Lizard Island and off Cairns. The Multi-barred Angelfish has also been observed in Indonesia, Borneo, Philippines, the Solomon Islands, and Tahiti. Until now, however, it has seldom been exported to North America and Europe.

155.
Centropyge multifasciatus
The specimen from the photo is 3.5 in. (9 cm) in length. This is probably the first underwater photo to be published of this fish.

155. ▼

Centropyge multispinis (PLAYFAIR, 1866)
Many-spined Angelfish

The presence of this species in Australia is questionable. The photo was taken of a specimen received by a Sydney pet dealer, and was presumably collected in the vicinity of Darwin. The Many-spined Angelfish is frequently encountered around the Maldive Islands and Sri Lanka, from where it is exported. This species is easily maintained in a tank, although it is very sensitive to copper treatment (in case of disease), which is true of all other angelfishes. The illustration shows a specimen of approximately 3.5 inches (9 cm) in length.

156 ▼

Centropyge nox (BLEEKER, 1853)
Midnight Angelfish

At New Guinea this species is usually encountered on outer reef slopes among rich coral growth, although it is occasionally sighted in lagoons and passages. It is quick to hide if approached by a diver. They are usually seen singly or in pairs at depths between 3–30 metres (10–100 ft.). The maximum size is about 3 inches (9 cm). Recently observed in Australia at Lizard Island.

The geographic range includes Melanesia, Indonesia, Philippines, Taiwan, Ryukyu Islands, and Japan. Exports are made to Europe and the USA from the Philippine Islands. Despite this, the Midnight Angelfish is seldom encountered in the home tank. It does not seem to be as popular as the more colourful members of the genus. This species thrives well in an algae-grown tank.

▼ 157

Centropyge tibicen (CUVIER, 1831)
Keyhole Angelfish

158 ▲ 159 ▼

The largest member of the genus, the Keyhole Angelfish attains a maximum length of 7 inches (18.5 cm). At Lord Howe Island large adults are common in shallow lagoon waters. It also occurs on coastal reefs in southern Queensland, New South Wales, Northern Territory, and off Western Australia. It is also found around the Moluccas, Philippines, New Hebrides, and throughout most of the Indo-Australian Archipelago. In the north the range extends to Taiwan and southern Japan. Like most members of the genus it is usually seen alone or in small aggregations. Adults tend to be bolder than other *Centropyge.* The shape of the white spot is extremely variable and at the onset of maturity, the yellow colouration on the fins becomes more pronounced.
Exports to the USA and Europe are not uncommon. Single specimens are easily kept in the aquarium.

158.
Centropyge tibicen
3 in. (7.5 cm).
This species thrives on a vegetable diet supplemented with frozen food. Keyhole Angelfish should not be kept together with other members of the family in the same tank as they are sometimes belligerent.

159.
Centropyge tibicen
The photo shows an almost adult specimen.
Aquarium photo.

Centropyge vroliki (BLEEKER, 1853)
Pearl-scaled Angelfish

The most common Centropyge found in the Australia-New Guinea region, *C. vroliki* inhabits lagoon and drop-off areas at depths from 1–25 metres (3–82 ft.). The species grows to 4 inches (10 cm) in length, at which stage the dark posterior area is outlined with vivid blue, as in *C. bispinosus.* However, the general colouration is drab by comparison with other angelfishes. This species is widespread in the Western Pacific, including Queensland, New South Wales, and New Guinea. In 1884, KLUNZINGER reported the Pearl-scaled Angelfish from the Red Sea. However, according to KLAUSEWITZ this statement was incorrect. *C. vroliki* is closely related to *C. flavissimus* and occasionally forms hybrids with this species (photo on the next page). Maintaining *C. vroliki* in a tank is not difficult compared with *C. flavissimus,* as the former species will accept food items other than algae.

160.
Centropyge vroliki
Underwater photo from the Great Barrier Reef, adult specimen, 4 in. (10 cm).

161.
Adult, 4 in. (10 cm), aquarium photo.

162.
Sub-adult specimen, 2.75 in. (7 cm), aquarium photo.

160 ▲

161 ▼

162 ▼

Centropyge vroliki x C. flavissimus

163 ▲ 164 ▼

The illustrated specimen is most likely a cross-breed between *C. vroliki* and *C. flavissimus.* Both photos were taken in an aquarium of a New York pet dealer. Similar specimens have been observed in the sea by ALLEN and RANDALL in the Marshall Islands, a locality where both presumed parents are known to occur.

According to RANDALL, ALLEN, and STEENE several species of butterflyfishes and angelfishes are known to form hybrids. It seems as though the hybridization potential is greater in species which are normally solitary or which form pairs in contrast to aggregating species. Perhaps if suitable males are in short supply the solitary fish seeks an individual of a closely related species for breeding.

There is little information about the breeding habits of angelfishes. Roger Lubbock of Cambridge University has observed spawning in a pair of *C. flavissimus.* The spawning took place near the bottom and was accompanied by slow swimming movements and physical contact between the participants. The eggs are tiny and transparent, and quickly float toward the surface after being released.

Genus
Chaetodontoplus

Chaetodontoplus mesoleucus

Chaetodontoplus ballinae WHITLEY, 1959
Ballina Angelfish

The fish pictured is the only specimen in existence and is deposited at the Australian Museum, Sydney. It was collected with a fish trap in deep water off Ballina, New South Wales in March, 1959. The colours of the fresh specimen were as follows: ground colour pearly grey with well defined dark areas mostly black; eye bright yellow; pectoral and caudal fins yellow, and remainder of fins pearly. Divers and fish collectors working in the North Solitary Islands of New South Wales have occasionally sighted a strange angelfish which is perhaps this species.
The maximum size of the Ballina Angelfish has not yet been determined. There are no data available on food requirements and the native habitat of this fish.
The yellow-brownish colouration of the illustrated specimen is due to its preservation in alcohol.

165 ▼

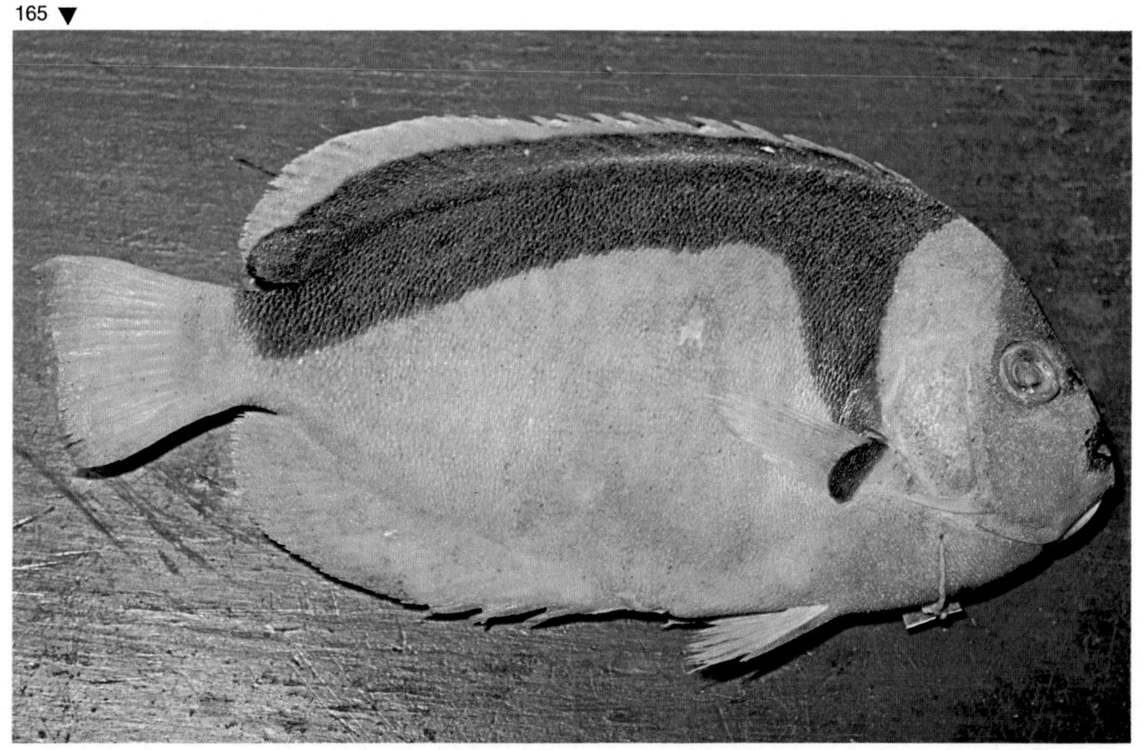

Chaetodontoplus conspicillatus (WAITE, 1900)
Conspicuous Angelfish

This species is most prevalent at Lord Howe Island, but has also been recorded from New Caledonia.
In addition, there is a questionable record from Heron Island, Great Barrier Reef. At Lord Howe Island it generally inhabits deep coral reef areas between 20 and 40 metres (66 and 130 ft.). However, one small individual was collected in the lagoon at a depth of only 2 metres (6 ft.). The maximum size attained is 10 inches (25.5 cm).
There are no records regarding the keeping of this species in a tank.

▼ 166

Chaetodontoplus duboulayi (GÜNTHER, 1867)
Scribbled Angelfish

Found on coastal and inner reefs of Queensland, Northern Territory, Western Australia, southern New Guinea and the Aru Islands. This species is usually found in small groups at depths between 1–20 metres (3–66 ft.). Juveniles, which are rarely encountered, are basically the same colour as adults. In some mature males the white patch behind the eye is more apparent. Specimens from the Darwin area seem to have a more elongate body shape than those found in Queensland. The maximum size is about 10 inches (25.5 cm).
The Scribbled Angelfish is highly prized as an aquarium fish. Unfortunately it is seldom exported except for large public show tanks.

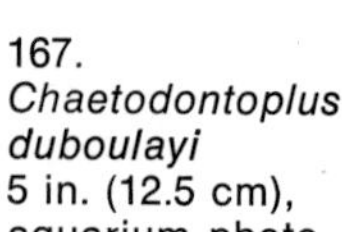

167.
Chaetodontoplus duboulayi
5 in. (12.5 cm),
aquarium photo.

168.
Chaetodontoplus duboulayi
Adult female,
8.6 in. (22 cm).

169.
Chaetodontoplus duboulayi
Male specimen,
8 in. (20 cm),
underwater photo from the Great Barrier Reef.

167 ▲ 168 ▼ 169 ▶

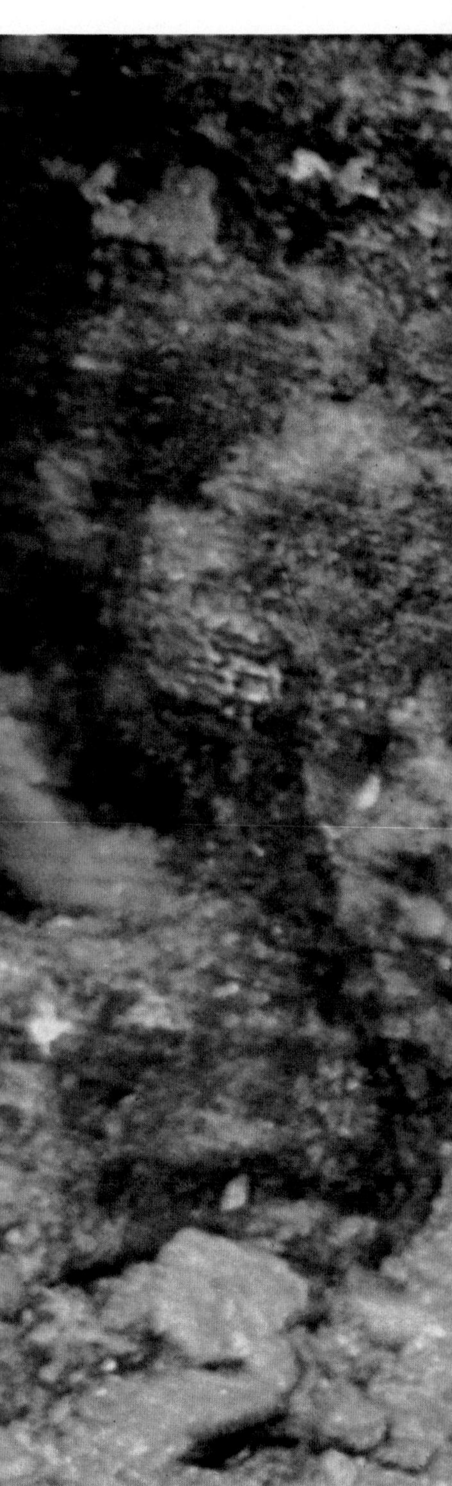

The keeping of this gorgeous species in an algae-tank, free of nitrate, is relatively easy. It is, however, difficult to obtain healthy specimens due to long transport distances. It is therefore recommended that only experienced hobbyists keep this fish. A variety of foods should be offered, including a vegetable diet.

Chaetodontoplus duboulayi on the Reef

Chaetodontoplus melanosoma (BLEEKER, 1853)

Black velvet Angelfish

170 ▲ 171 ▼

This species has not yet been recorded from Australia but has been collected under the wharf at Samarai Island, off the eastern tip of New Guinea. It attains a maximum length of 7 inches (18 cm). BLEEKER described a separate species, *Holacanthus dimidiatus,* which is similar in appearance, but has the caudal fin entirely yellow. According to FRASER-BRUNNER this merely represents the female colour form of *C. melanosoma.* The juveniles, as with most angelfishes, have a characteristic colour pattern which differs from that of the adults. Specimens under about 2.5 inches (6 cm) have a curved yellow bar as shown in the drawing; the ground colour is uniformly black. The Black velvet Angelfish adapts well to life in an aquarium.

170.
Chaetodontoplus melanosoma
Sub-adult,
4.25 in. (11 cm),
aquarium photo.

171.
Chaetodontoplus melanosoma
Adult, 6 in. (15 cm).

Chaetodontoplus mesoleucus (BLOCH, 1787)
Vermiculated Angelfish

At first glance this species looks like a butterflyfish (genus Chaetodon), but it possesses the characteristic spine on the cheek which is typical for all angelfishes. It has not been recorded from Australia but from the coastal waters of New Guinea, Indonesia, and the Philippines at depths from 2–20 metres (6–66 ft.). This species is generally solitary in habit and easy to approach. Adults attain a length of 7 inches (18 cm). The Vermiculated Angelfish slightly resembles *Holacanthus xanthurus;* there is, however, a scale difference. *C. mesoleucus* has 85 or more scales along the lateral line, while *H. xanthurus* has less than 50. The Vermiculated Angel is a fish for the experienced hobbyist only. Food requirements consist of vegetable matter as well as small animal food.

172 ▲ 173 ▼

172.
Chaetodontoplus mesoleucus
Adult, 6 in. (15 cm), underwater photo from New Guinea.

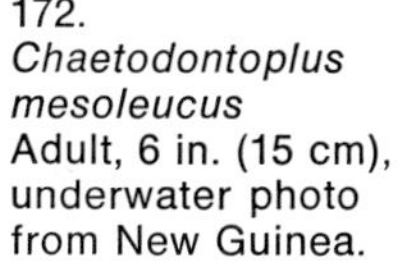

173.
Chaetodontoplus mesoleucus
Sub-adult, 4 in. (10 cm), aquarium photo.

Chaetodontoplus personifer (McCULLOCH, 1914)
Yellow-tail Angelfish

This is not a common species, at least in the sea off northern Queensland where it is found on inner and coastal reefs. It occurs on the Great Barrier Reef proper further south at the Capricorn Group and on the Pompey and Swains Reefs. It has also been recorded from Western Australia and New South Wales. The juveniles have dark head markings which gradually change to the characteristic blue pattern of adults; in addition, they have a broad white bar above the gills. The Yellow-tail Angel is extremely inquisitive and will readily approach a diver. It is generally seen alone or in small aggregations. The maximum size attained is 10 inches (25.5 cm).

174 ▲ 175 ▼

174. *Chaetodontoplus personifer* Juvenile, 2.5 in. (6 cm), aquarium photo. The markings of the juveniles differ considerably from the adults. There are no records at the disposal of the author regarding the tank life of this species. However, photographs from the USA indicate that the fish has been imported to this country. The food requirements of the Yellow-tail Angelfish should be similar to those of the other angelfishes.

175. *Chaetodontoplus personifer* Adult, 9 in. (23 cm), underwater photo.

Genus
Euxiphipops

Euxiphipops sextriatus

Euxiphipops navarchus (CUVIER, 1831)
Blue-girdled Angelfish

The angels are among the most exotic of all fishes and this species is certainly no exception. The magnificently coloured Blue-girdled Angelfish retains the same colour pattern throughout most its life-span. Only the smallest individuals have different markings. It is a common fish in certain areas of New Guinea, frequenting protected lagoons and drop-off areas with heavy coral growth at depths between 3 and 30 metres (10 and 100 ft.). They generally occur solitarily and are relatively easy to approach. The maximum length attained is about 10 inches (25.5 cm). Recently observed at Rowley Shoals, Western Australia. Additionally, the geographic range includes the entire Indo-Australian Archipelago. Exports to the USA and Europe usually originate from the Philippines. Young specimens, undamaged in transport, adapt readily to tank life. After a short period of acclimation they will accept flake food from their owner's hand.

176. *Euxiphipops navarchus* Sub-adult, 6 in. (15 cm), underwater photo from New Guinea.

177. Until they have attained a length of 1.5 in. (4 cm), juveniles are easily confused with those of *P. annularis*, which – on the contrary – have a whitish caudal fin.

178. *Euxiphipops navarchus* 2 in. (5 cm). Juveniles have a dark-blue ground colour with bright-blue stripes, an orange dorsal and a transparent caudal fin. Aquarium photo.

◄ 176 177 ▲ 178 ▼

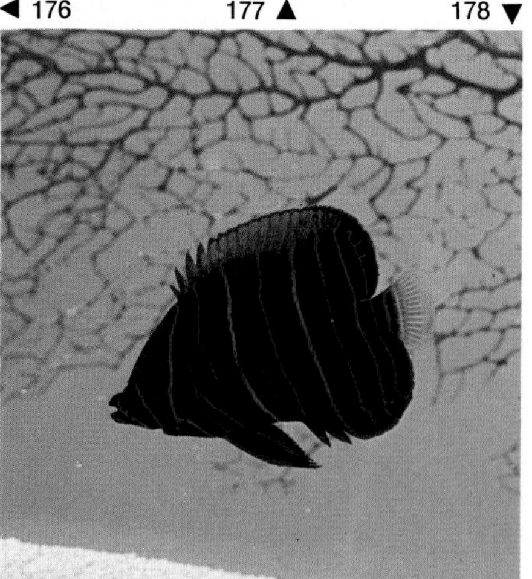

Euxiphipops sexstriatus (CUVIER, 1831)
Six-banded Angelfish

This species is perhaps the most common of the large angels inhabiting the Australia-New Guinea region. In Australia this species is known from Queensland and Western Australia. Other localities include the Solomon Islands, Philippines, and southern Indonesia. In the vicinity of Green Island on the Great Barrier Reef, this species has a density of approximately 20 pairs per thousand square metres, at depths ranging from 2–5 metres (6–16 ft.). The juveniles look very similar to the young of *Pomacanthus semicirculatus,* but the white body bars are vertical whereas on *semicirculatus* they are curved. The adults are found mostly in pairs and are quick to seek shelter when approached by a diver. When harrassed this species has the unusual habit of emitting a loud grunting sound. Several other angelfishes also exhibit this trait. The maximum size is from 12–18 inches (30.5–45.5 cm). Because of its enormous size only the young are exported. The adults of the Six-banded Angelfish are not suited for the home aquarium as the large size precludes proper aquarium management. The young however, make excellent aquarium fish.

179.
Euxiphipops sexstriatus
Juvenile,
3 in. (8 cm).

179 ▲

180.
Euxiphipops sexstriatus
Sub-adult specimen, still showing the vertical blue head bars of the juvenile.
4 in. (10 cm).
Aquarium photo.

180 ▼

Euxiphipops sexstriatus x xanthometapon

This illustration shows another hybrid angelfish, probably *E. sexstriatus x E. xanthometapon.* The specimen in question is almost adult and has a length of 10 inches (25 cm). It was collected by using a multi-prong spear, hence the damage in the gill area.
This specimen was collected at Michaelmas Reef, Queensland, in 12 metres (40 ft.) on 10-10-1975. It was seen in company with an adult *E. sexstriatus* of the same size. Several pairs of both parent species were observed nearby.
Two other Angelfish hybrids have been reported to date, from the Caribbean Sea, as well as the crossing between *C. vroliki* and *C. flavissimus* (see page 110).

182.
Euxiphipops sexstriatus
Adult, 12 in. (30 cm).
Underwater photo from the Barrier Reef.

181 ▼

182 ▶

Euxiphipops sexstriatus on the Reef

Euxiphipops xanthometapon (BLEEKER, 1853)
Yellow-faced Angelfish

The exotic Yellow-faced Angelfish is not often seen in the Australia-New Guinea region. The adults, which reach 15 inches (38 cm) in length, are found adjacent to steep drop-offs or in protected lagoons at depths ranging from 5—20 metres (16—66 ft.). They are solitary in habit. The Australian portion of the range includes Queensland and Western Australia. The species also occurs throughout Indonesia, north-western Melanesia, and western Micronesia.
The Yellow-faced Angelfish is regularly offered by Philippine dealers and also from Singapore. Specimens under 4—8 inches (10—20 cm) in length are best adapted to tank life. The hobbyist should bear in mind, however, that this is a fish for the experienced aquarist only.

183 ▲

184 ▼

Head of the Yellow-faced Angelfish
Euxiphipops xanthometapon

▼ 185

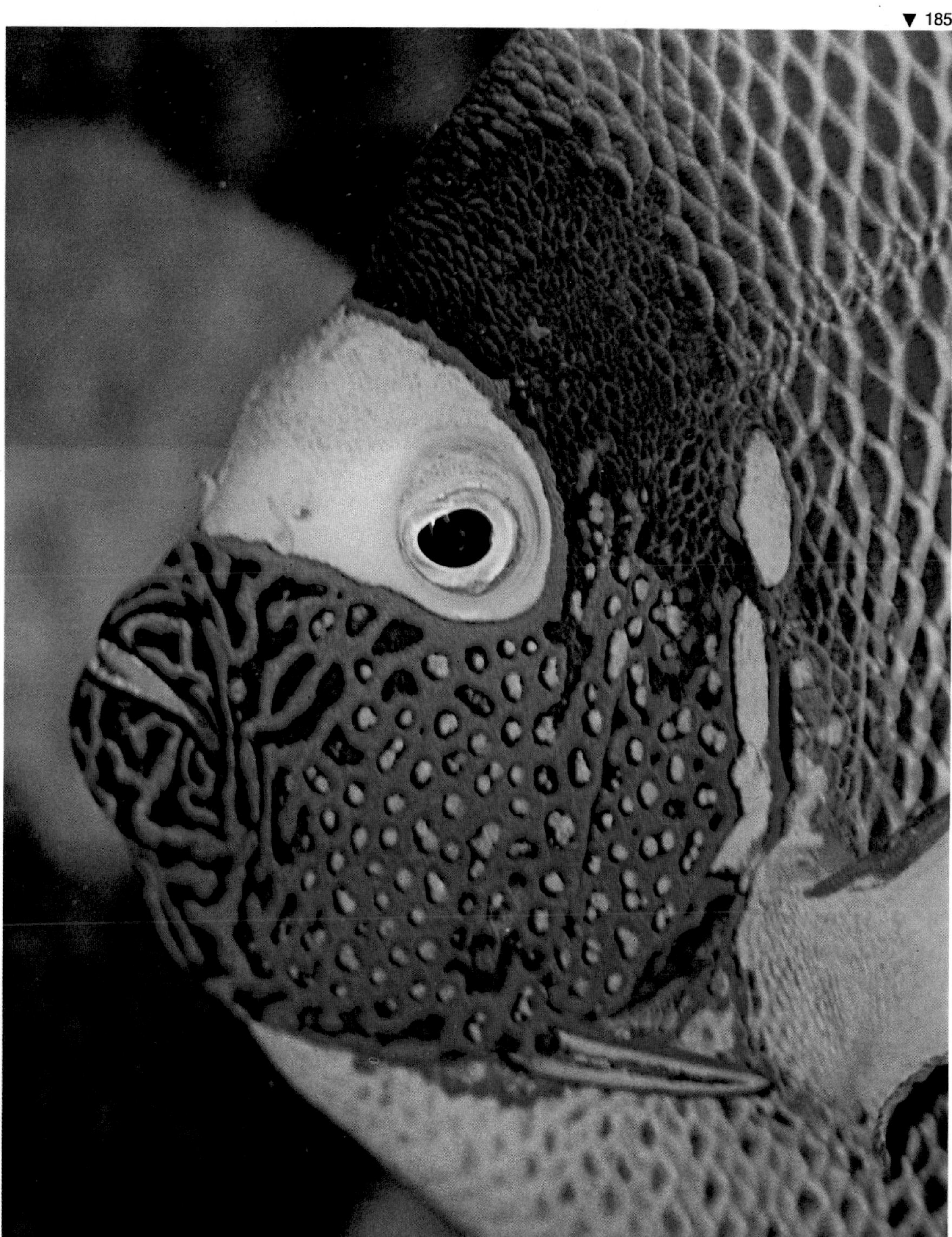

183.
Euxiphipops xanthometapon
Juvenile,
3 in. (7.5 cm).

184.
Euxiphipops xanthometapon
Adult, 10 in. (25 cm).

Genus
Genicanthus

Genicanthus lamarck

Genicanthus lamarck (LACÉPÈDE, 1802)
Lamarck's Angelfish

The Genicanthus angels are the most poorly known members of the family, mainly because most species inhabit deep reefs adjacent to steep slopes. Apparently these fishes exist on a diet which includes a large percentage of planktonic items. They occur in small to large aggregations which are commonly observed feeding in midwater well above the bottom. Members of this group exhibit remarkable differences in colouration between the male and female. This characteristic has created confusion among fish taxonomists and the different sexes have invariably been described as separate species. However, modern diving techniques allowing biologists to explore the deeper reefs have enabled them to visually link the male and female forms. For example the sexes of this species differ in pelvic and caudal fin colouration. In addition, males have a bright yellow spot on the forehead and more elongate caudal filaments. The maximum size is about 9 inches (23 cm). Several individuals of *G. lamarck* were found in an unusual habitat near the wharf at Samarai, New Guinea, in only 10 metres (33 ft.). Inhabitants of the Moluccas regard this fish as a delicacy. This is a rare species in the Western Pacific ranging from the Solomon Islands and the New Hebrides northward to Japan. Lamarck's Angelfish is restless and shy in the aquarium. They are seldom exported, therefore there is little information available about their maintenance. Nevertheless, it is possible to keep adults in a tank that is more than 1.2 metres (4 ft.) in length and furnished with ample hiding spaces. They are normally plankton-eaters and will accept fine, free-floating food. The aquarist must supplement their diet with frozen and flake food, and freeze-dried items of good quality (no tubifex!).

186 ▲ 187 ▼

▼ 188

186. *Genicanthus lamarck* Adult female, 3.75 in. (9.5 cm), standard length.

187. *Genicanthus lamarck* Adult male, 4.6 in. (11.7 cm), standard length.

188. *Genicanthus lamarck* Female specimen, 3.5 in. (9 cm), aquarium photo.

Genicanthus melanospilos (BLEEKER, 1857)
Black-spot Angelfish

The male and female forms of this species differ greatly as illustrated in the photos. The male is characterized by a series of dark bands on the side and large black spot ventrally on the middle of the breast (hence the name *melanospilos* meaning "black-spot"). The two sexes are always found together in water at least 20 metres (66 ft.) deep. They have been recorded from the Great Barrier Reef off Cairns and at Madang and Rabaul in areas of rich coral growth interspersed with sand. The female form was formerly described as *G. macclesfieldiensis.* The maximum length is about 7 inches (18 cm). This species is widespread in the Western Pacific Ocean. In the Red Sea and Western Indian Ocean there is a closely related species, *G. caudovittatus.* Care and maintenance is similar to that recommended for *G. lamarck.* Both species are sometimes exported to the USA but are seldom seen in European tanks.

189. *Genicanthus melanospilos* Adult male specimen, 7 in. (18 cm), underwater photo.

190. *Genicanthus melanospilos* Sub-adult female specimen, 3.5 in. (9 cm), underwater photo.

191. Adult male specimen. This fish lacks the extended spines of the dorsal and caudal fin, which might be due to shipping damage.

192. Aquarium photo of a female specimen, 5 in. (12.5 cm).

189 ▲

190 ▲

191 ▼

192 ▼

Genicanthus semicinctus (WAITE, 1900)
Half-banded Angelfish

This species is known only from Lord Howe Island. It inhabits deep coral reef areas to depths of at least 40 metres (130 ft.). A significant difference in colour exists between male and female. The males possess a series of dark bands on the sides. Most of the known specimens of *Genicanthus semicinctus* were collected by the 1973 expedition to Lord Howe Island sponsored by the National Geographic Society and the Australian Museum. The female form was unknown prior to this expedition.
The subject of male-female colour differences is a fascinating one. It is difficult to understand why sexes are frequently so different in colour. No doubt the differences aid intraspecific sex recognition and perhaps the bright male colours serve as a stimulant which attracts females in reproductive condition. Apparently this species has never been maintained in home aquaria.

193 ▲

194 ▼

193. *Genicanthus semicinctus* Adult female, 5 in. (12.5 cm), underwater photo.

194. *Genicanthus semicinctus* Adult male, 7 in. (18 cm), underwater photo.

Genicanthus watanabei (YASUDA and TOMINAGA, 1970)
Watanabe's Angelfish

This is a rare species in the Australia-New Guinea region. The only reliable record is based on specimens collected in 1972 at Osprey Reef off the northern Queensland coast. These individuals were found at depths between 60 and 70 metres (200–230 ft.) on the steep outer reef-slope. There is also an unconfirmed report of a sighting at Langford Island near Hayman Island (Queensland), on the edge of a steep drop-off. The geographic range extends from New Caledonia northward to southern Japan. The male and female exhibit significant differences in colouration with the former sex being much more ornate.

Very little is known about the aquarium maintenance of this species because of the lack of imports. Captured specimens frequently suffer from damage due to improper decompression times when collected.

195.
Genicanthus watanabei
Sub-adult female, 4 in. (10 cm), underwater photo.

196.
Genicanthus watanabei
Adult female, 4.3 in. (10.9 cm), standard length.

197.
Genicanthus watanabei
Adult male, 6 in. (15 cm), underwater photo from the Great Barrier Reef.

198.
Genicanthus watanabei
Male, 4.5 in. (11.5 cm), standard length. The yellow bar, extending from the middle of the body to the caudal peduncle is clearly visible.

195 ▲

196 ▲

197 ▼

198 ▼

Genus
Pomacanthus

Pomacanthus imperator

Pomacanthus annularis (BLOCH, 1787)

Blue-ringed Angelfish

This species is apparently rare. Only one specimen has been observed in the region covered by this book. It was seen under the main wharf at Madang, New Guinea, at a depth of 15 metres (50 ft.). This species attains a length of 12 inches (30.5 cm) and undergoes a complete colour transformation from the juvenile to adult stage.

The Blue-ringed Angelfish ranges from Sri Lanka (formerly Ceylon) eastward to the Solomon Islands. Regular exports to the USA and Europe, primarily from Ceylon, have made this beautiful Angelfish one of the most popular salt-water tank fish. Among the large angelfishes, however, it is one of the more delicate species (except for *Pygoplites).*

199 ▲ 200 ▼

199.
Pomacanthus annularis
The specimen in the illustration shows the typical juvenile colour pattern characteristic of all large angels. Size 2.75 in. (7 cm). Juveniles are easily confused with *P. chrysurus,* but lack the yellow caudal fin of the latter.

200.
Pomacanthus annularis
Sub-adult, 7 in. (18 cm), aquarium photo. This Angelfish prefers a large algae tank with ample hiding places and will accept any kind of food. Live food, however, is preferred. If a "newcomer" refuses to eat the aquarist should offer it "feeding-stones".

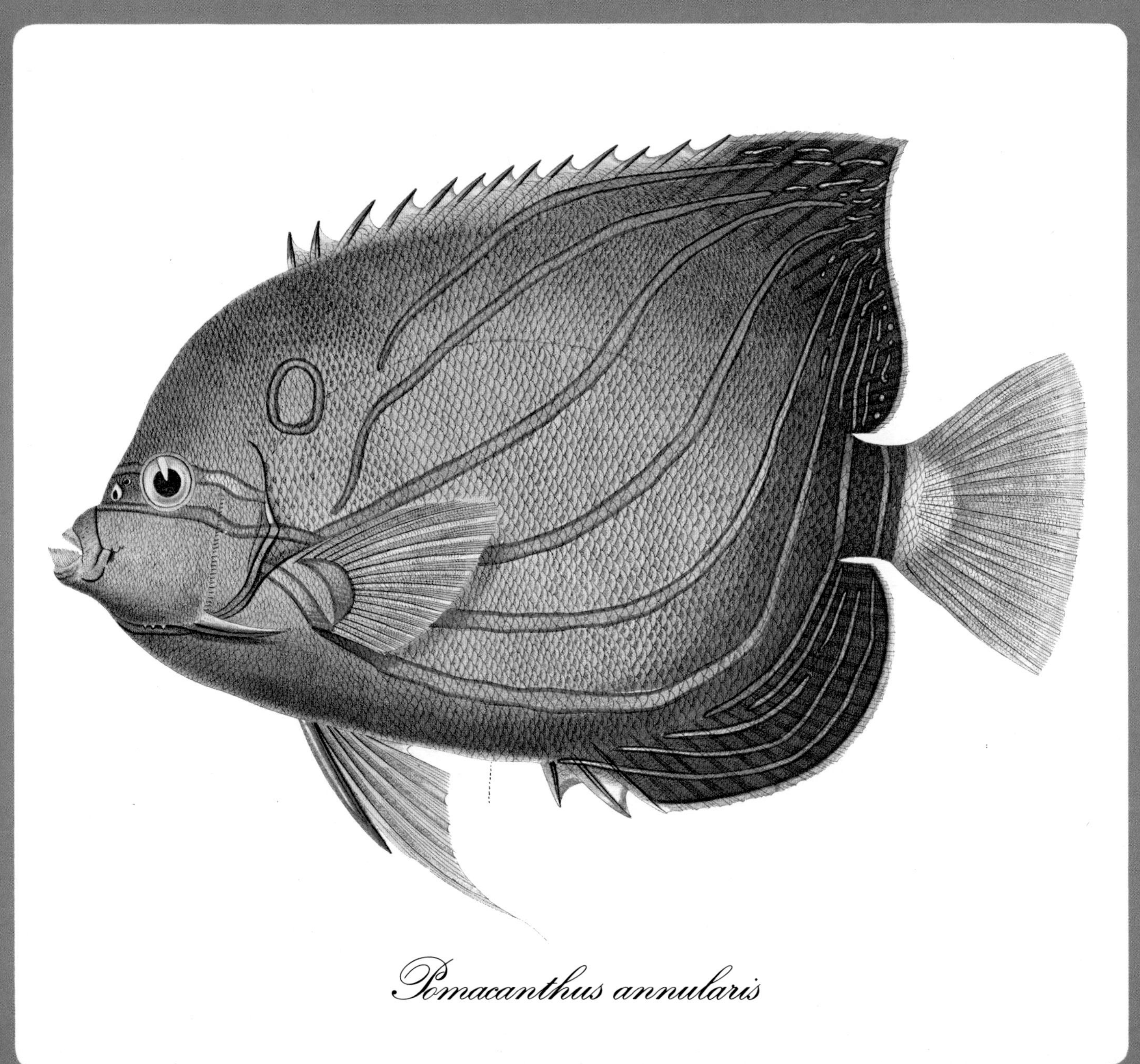

Pomacanthus annularis

Pomacanthus imperator (BLOCH, 1787)
Emperor Angelfish

The Emperor Angel is found almost exclusively on outer reefs of live coral. It is common on northern sections of the Great Barrier Reef and also at New Guinea in depths between 1 and 25 metres (3–82 ft.). In addition, it is widespread from the Red Sea and East Africa to Hawaii, although only one specimen has been collected at the latter locality. Generally, the Emperor Angel is found singly, but it also occurs in pairs or trios. A dramatic colour change takes place from the juvenile to the adult form. The young are dark blue with a series of concentric white rings. Mature individuals are characterized by a pointed extension of the soft dorsal fin. The

201 ▲ 202 ▼

201. *Pomacanthus imperator* Juvenile, 3 in. (7.5 cm), aquarium photo. Juveniles of *P. imperator* differ considerably from the young of other large angels as this is the only species in which the white markings of the posterior part of the body form a ring.

202. *Pomacanthus imperator* Sub-adult, 4 in. (10 cm). Specimen in transition stage. Aquarium photo.

204. *Pomacanthus imperator* Adult, 10 in. (25 cm). Underwater photo from the Great Barrier Reef.

maximum size is about 12 inches (30.5 cm). The Emperor Angel is a sturdy aquarium species; when offered a variety of foods, they have been known to live more than five years in captivity. The species is belligerent toward fish of their own kind as well as towards other large angelfishes. Until 1933, the juvenile form was regarded as a separate species, which was called *P. nicobariensis.* The markings of the juvenile from the East African coast shown in illustration 203 deviate slightly from the normal form (illustration 201). It is not certain if this unusual pattern is found in all young specimens from this region.

203 ▲

204 ▼

Pomacanthus semicirculatus (CUVIER, 1831)
Semicircle Angelfish

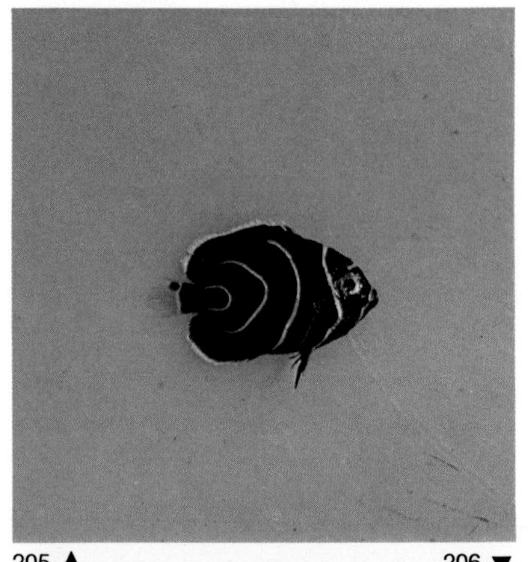

205 ▲

This is another angelfish which exhibits a dramatic colour change during its life cycle. The young look very similar to juvenile *Euxiphopops sexstriatus* and are often confused with that species. The range includes Queensland, Western Australia, New South Wales, and New Guinea. It is also widespread over the Indian Ocean, from South Africa, Mauritius, Seychelles, the Red Sea, and Sri Lanka, eastward to Indonesia and the Western Pacific from New Caledonia, Fiji, and Samoa, northward to Japan. Generally the Semicircle Angel frequents depths less than 25 metres (82 ft.). The juveniles are mostly found in shallow water on top of reefs where there is a large percentage of sandy bottom. Very small individuals are confined to dark caverns and are seldom seen.

205.–209. *Pomacanthus semicirculatus* Juvenile specimens of different sizes:
0.6 in. (1.7 cm) (205)
1.75 in. (4.5 cm) (206)
2.5 in. (6.0 cm) (207)
4.0 in. (10 cm) (208)
6.9 in. (17.5 cm) (209)
Sub-adult specimen, just beginning to change colours.

206 ▼

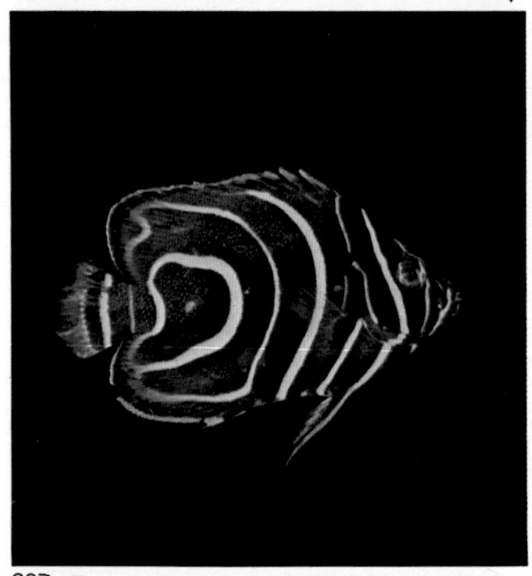

207 ▼

208 ▲

209 ▼

210. *Pomacanthus semicirculatus* Adult, 12 in. (30 cm), underwater photo from the Great Barrier Reef.

Adults prefer protected areas with heavy coral growth which offer ample hiding places. They are generally solitary in occurence. The maximum size is 15 inches (38 cm). The juvenile illustrated in photo 205, only 17 mm (0.6 inches) in length, is possibly the smallest specimen ever collected. It was taken with rotenone in 30 metres (100 ft.) at Madang, New Guinea. Aquarium care is similar to that recommended for other angelfishes. The young make excellent aquarium fish and are suitable for a community tank.

▼ 210

Genus: *Pygoplites*

Pygoplites diacanthus (BODDAERT, 1772)
Regal Angelfish

One of the more common pomacanthids on the Great Barrier Reef, the Regal Angelfish is found in areas which abound with holes and crevices. It is also recorded from New Guinea and Western Australia, and ranges widely in the Indo-Pacific from the Red Sea and eastern Africa eastward to Tahiti. They are mainly collected for export from the coastal waters of Manila, Singapore, and Sri Lanka. The species prefers rich coral areas under the influence of currents and moderate wave action. The depth range is from 1 to 20 metres (3–66 ft.). It generally occurs singly but is sometimes seen in pairs. These fish are always on the move, going from crevice to crevice. Juveniles are found deep in sheltered caverns and have the same basic colouration as adults except for the presence of a spot on the soft dorsal fin which disappears with growth. The adults attain a length of 10 inches (25.5 cm). The Regal Angelfish is a finicky eater and therefore very difficult to maintain in captivity for any length of time. Usually it dies within six months or so and it is therefore recommended that only experienced aquarists with large show tanks attempt to keep it. The food should include a large variety of both animal and plant matter.

211 ▲ 212 ▼ 213 ▶

211.
Pygoplites diacanthus
Juvenile,
1.4 in. (3.5 cm),
aquarium photo.

212.
Pygoplites diacanthus
Juvenile,
3 in. (7.5 cm),
underwater photo.

213.
Pygoplites diacanthus
Underwater photo of an adult specimen, 7 in. (18 cm).
New Guinea.

Index of common names

Index of scientific names

* These species do not occur around Australia and New Guinea.

Literature cited

Ahl, E. 1923. Zur Kenntnis der Knochenfischfamilie Chaetodontidae, insbesondere der Unterfamilie Chaetodontinae. Arch. Naturg. A 89 (5): 1–205.

Allen, G. R. and D. F. Hoese, J. R. Paxton, J. E. Randall, B. C. Russell, W. A. Starck II, F. H. Talbot and G. P. Whitley 1976. Annotated checklist of the Fishes of Lord Howe Island. Rec. Aust. Mus. 30 (15) 365–454.

Allen, G. R. 1969. The stripey. Trop. Fish Hobbyist. 18 (November): 86–87.

Baensch, H. A.; 1975. Kleine Seewasser Praxis, Tetra Verlag, Melle.

Bagnis, R. and P. Mazellier, J. Bennett and E. Christian, 1974. Fishes of Polynesia, Lansdowne Press, Victoria.

Burgess, W. E. 1974. Evidence for the elevation to family status of the angelfishes (Pomacanthidae), previously considered to be a sub-family of the butterflyfish family Chaetodontidae. Pac. Sci., 28 (1): 57–71.

Burgess, W. E. and H. R. Axelrod, 1972–1976. Pacific Marine Fishes, Books 1–6. T. F. H. Pub. Inc. New Jersey.

Cuvier, G. and A. Valenciennes, 1831. Histoire Naturelle des Poissons, Leurault, Paris.

de Graaf, F. 1969. Das Tropische Meerwasseraquarium. Verlag J. Neumann-Neudamm, Melsungen.

Ehrlich, P. R., F. H. Talbot, B. C. Russell and G. R. V. Anderson. 1977. The behaviour of chaetodontid fishes with special reference to Lorenz's "poster colouration hypothesis". J. Zool. Lond. 183: 213–228.

Goldman, B. 1967. Chaetodon aphrodite, the juvenile of Chaetodon flavirostris (Teleostei, Chaetodontidae). Proc. Roy. Zool. Soc. N. S. Wales 1965–66 (1967) 45–51.

Gosline, W. A. and V. E. Brock, 1960. Handbook of Hawaiian Fishes. Uni. of Hawaii Press, Honolulu.

Grant, E. 1972. Guide to Fishes Dept. of Primary Industries, Qld.

Hiatt, R. W., and D. W. Strasburg. 1960. Ecological relationships of the fish fauna on coral reefs of the Marshall Islands. Ecol. Monogr., 30:65–127.

Hobson, E., and E. H. Chave. 1972. Hawaiian Reef Animals.

Klausewitz, W. 1975. Handbuch der Meeres-Aquaristik, Fische I. Engelbert Pfriem Verlag, Wuppertal-Elberfeld.

Marshall, T. 1966. Tropical Fishes of the Great Barrier Reef. Angus and Robertson, Sydney.

Munro, I. S. R. 1967. The Fishes of New Guinea. Dept. of Agriculture, Stock and Fisheries, Port Moresby, New Guinea.

Randall, J. E. 1975. A revision of the Indo-Pacific angelfish genus Genicanthus, with descriptions of three new species. Bull. Mar. Sci. 25 (3):393–421.

Randall, J. E., G. R. Allen, and R. C. Steene. Five probable hybrid butterflyfishes of the genus Chaetodon from the Central and Western Pacific. Rec. West. Aust. Mus.

Randall, J. E. and D. K. Caldwell. 1970. Clarification of the species of the butterflyfish genus Forcipiger. Copeia No. 4. 727–731.

Randall, J. E. and R. C. Wass. 1974. Two new pomacanthid fishes of the genus Centropyge from Oceania. Japan. J. Ichthyol. 21 (3) 137–144.

Reese, E. S. 1973. Duration of residence by coral reef fishes on home reefs. Copeia No. 1. 145–149.

Slastenenko, E. P. 1957. A list of natural fish hybrids of the world. Hidrobiologi, ser: B, 4 (2–3) : 76–97.

Smith, J. L. B. 1965. The Sea Fishes of southern Africa. Central News Agency, South Africa.

Smith, J. L. B. and M. M. Smith. 1969. The Fishes of Seychelles. The J. L. B. Smith Inst. of Ichthyology, Grahamstown, South Africa.

Stead, D. G. 1906. Fishes of Australia. William Brooks & Co., Limited, Sydney.

The Philippine Journal of Science 1927–59. Ichthyological Papers, Vol. 2. Articles 31–59.

Weber, M. and L. F. De Beaufort. 1936. The Fishes of the Indo-Australian Archipelago Vol. VII.

Whitley, G. P. 1959. More ichthyological snippets. Proc. Roy. Soc. N. S. W. 1957–58:11–26.

Whitley, G. P. 1964. Presidential Address. A. survey of Australian Ichthyology. Proc. Linn. Soc. N. S. W., 89 (1):11–127.

Woods, L. P. and L. P. Schultz. 1953. Subfamily Pomacanthinae. IN L. P. Schultz et al., Fishes of the Marshall and Marianas Islands. Bull. U. S. Nat. Mus., 202 (1):597–608.

Map of the Australia-New Guinea region.

Photo Credits

Author (107): 2, 4, 5, 6, 7, 9, 11, 12, 13, 14, 15, 17, 18, 19, 20, 21, 24, 28, 30, 32–34, 35, 39, 41, 43, 44, 46, 47, 48, 51, 52, 53, 55, 56, 58, 60, 62, 67, 70, 73, 74, 76, 77, 78, 79, 81, 83, 84, 85, 89, 90, 91, 93, 94, 97, 98, 100, 101, 102, 105, 106, 107, 108, 110, 113, 114, 117, 118, 120, 121, 123, 124, 127, 128, 130, 132, 134, 141, 142, 152, 155, 158, 160, 165, 168, 169, 172, 175, 176, 179, 181, 182, 184, 185, 189, 190, 195, 197, 205, 206, 209, 210, 212, 213, 2 title photos

Dr. Gerald R. Allen (6): 57, 61, 122, 148, 193, 194

Hans A. Baensch (1): 71

John Butler (2): 87, 88

Helmut Debelius (3): 136 a/b, 211

Wade Doak (3): 22, 86, 166

Peter Erbe (1): 80

Dr. Robert Goldstein (1): 154

Rodney S. L. Jonklaas (1): 10

Burkard Kahl (3): 37, 68, 126

Earl Kennedy (2): 177, 178

Rudie H. Kuiter (15): 3, 29, 69, 82, 118 b, 133, 140, 144, 147, 150, 156, 157, 171, 183, 199

Roger Lubbock (1): 109

Horst Moosleitner (1): 65

Aaron Norman (51): 1, 8, 23, 25, 36, 38, 40, 42, 50, 54, 59, 63, 66, 72, 75, 92, 96, 99, 103, 111, 112, 115, 118 a, 119, 125, 129, 131, 138, 139, 143, 145, 146, 149, 151, 153, 162, 163, 164, 167, 170, 173, 174, 180, 188, 191, 192, 200, 201, 202, 207, 208

Arend van den Nieuwenhuizen (12): 16, 26, 27, 45, 49, 64, 95, 116, 135, 137, 159, 161

Roy O'Connor (2): 204, 1 title photo Genicanthus

Steve Parish (1): 104

Dr. John Randall (5): 31, 186, 187, 196, 198

Vince Vlasoff (1): p. 2/3

Herwarth Voigtmann (1): 203

The colour fish drawings are taken from Pieter Bleeker's "Atlas of Indo-Malayan Fishes", 1876/77.

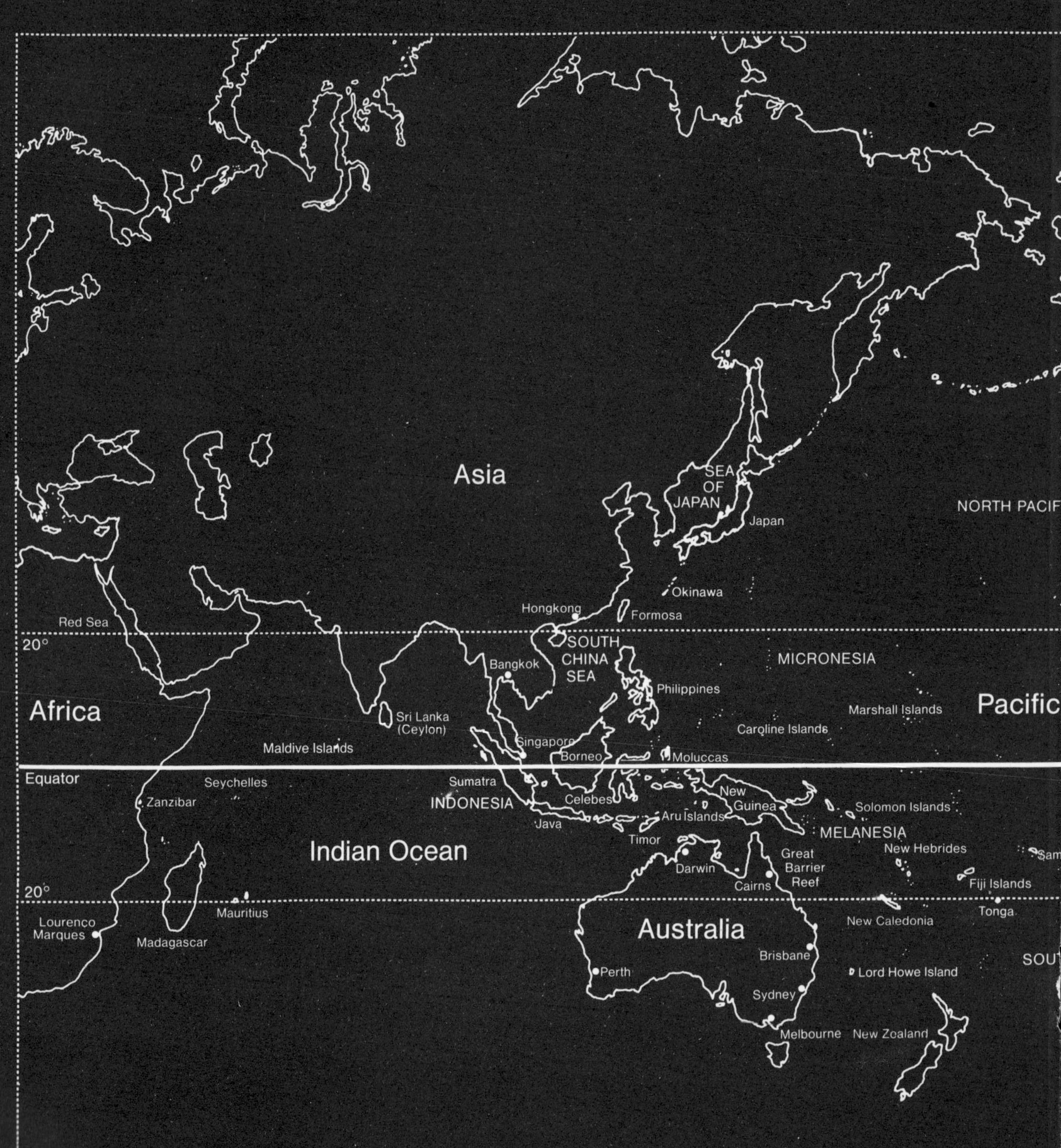
Asia
SEA
OF
JAPAN
Japan
NORTH PACIF
Okinawa
Hongkong
Formosa
Red Sea
20°
SOUTH
CHINA
SEA
MICRONESIA
Bangkok
Philippines
Africa
Sri Lanka
(Ceylon)
Marshall Islands
Pacific
Caroline Islands
Maldive Islands
Singapore
Borneo
Moluccas
Equator
Seychelles
Sumatra
Zanzibar
INDONESIA
Celebes
New
Guinea
Solomon Islands
Aru Islands
Java
MELANESIA
Indian Ocean
Timor
Great
Barrier
Reef
New Hebrides
Darwin
Cairns
20°
Fiji Islands
Mauritius
Tonga
Lourenco
Marques
Madagascar
Australia
New Caledonia
Brisbane
Perth
Lord Howe Island
Sydney
Melbourne
New Zealand